T0098440

I, Eric Ngalle

Eric Ngalle was born in Cameroon. He has travelled widely, including a period living in Russia where he learned Russian while attempting to seek sanctuary. He eventually reached Wales, where he was able to live and work. He studied modern history and popular culture at Cardiff Metropolitan University and obtained a Creative Wales Award from the Arts Council of Wales for his research in migration, memory and trauma. His work has been featured by the BBC and performed at the Hay Literature Festival. He lives in Cardiff and works as a writer and performer.

I, Eric Ngalle

One man's journey crossing
continents from Africa
to Europe

Eric Ngalle

Parthian
www.parthianbooks.com
First published in 2019
Reprinted 2021
© Eric Ngalle 2019
ISBN 978-1-912109-10-4
British Library Cataloguing in Publication Data
A cataloguing record for this book is available from the British Library.

For my mother, my daughter and her sisters,
this is how I came to be here in Wales.

Prologue

I was not of this earth as I stood – petrol can in one hand and box of matches in the other –and gazed with hatred upon my late father's house through dead eyes; a darkness in my soul and intent in my heart. The night carried no sound, as though it were holding its breath, and even the moon could not bear to watch and hid behind angry clouds, the likes of which seldom trouble African skies.

I had been rejected and I felt humiliated; this was the day I prayed and wished for death, for the devil had placed his hands deep down my throat and into my stomach, I had been disembowelled, my entrails dropped to the ground and stampeded upon. I knew that people – my people, my kin – lay asleep under that roof but I prepared myself to douse the walls with petrol and strike a match to entice the flames to rear up into a dance of destruction.

I did not care about being seen – whether by any of the villagers or even the ghosts of my ancestors who live on the periphery of this world – for I was certain my soul had died and Satan had flown away with me; I had become the devil himself.

Who dares to make my mother cry? My sisters, my aunts, my uncles? They were all marked. I had placed a curse on them and their household; I had issued them with a fatwa. Now was the time to act.

But as I took a step forward, ready to set the wheels in motion that would carry me to damnation, the soothing voice of my mother reached out through the night, caressed my ears and entered my thoughts. I turned and walked towards home but there were no signs of a new dawn seeping through the darkness – my mother's words may have halted my actions but my day of reckoning would surely come. I, Eric Ngalle Charles, would have my revenge in this life and not wait for the next.

1

Chapter 1

Arriving in Russia

I grew up in the village of Wovilla near Small Soppo in the shadow of Mount Cameroon. I had Africa in my blood but on passing my A-levels all I wanted to do was get the hell out of Cameroon—it was the only avenue open to me if I wanted to build myself a better life. With my father gone—along with any inheritance—and my mother being poor, the only way I could make this happen was through state sponsorship or a scholarship to a foreign university.

I had turned to the internet and contacted a Canadian immigration lawyer who said he had links to several universities and could advise on sponsorship and how I could study abroad. I eventually applied to two universities, one in Ontario, Canada, and the other in Bruges, Belgium. The first to offer me a place was the university in Belgium. I was very excited as it offered a way forward following the horror of being robbed of my inheritance and being on the point of committing murder—yet here I was on my way to the land of milk and honey. The university's offer, which was genuine and offered me a chance to study economics, was the only thing that could have rescued me.

My mother gave me what little money she could spare and I made my way to the capital, Yaoundé and then to Bastos, where all the embassies are situated, to finalise my travel arrangements—and yet to this day I haven't been to the Belgium Embassy.

Fortunately my sister lived in Yaoundé, so I had somewhere to stay, and the next day I made my way to Bastos and sat in a café where I was to meet an embassy official, or so I was led to believe.

All around us people were talking about flying off to study in this university or that university in places around the world—I didn't realise at the time but this was all part of a plan to lure me in.

The embassy official took my passport and the small amount of money that I had managed to scrape together and disappeared telling me someone would be in touch soon. The next contact I had was with a different 'embassy official'—he was so horrible he even came to where I was staying and dated my sister. I had fallen into the hands of human traffickers and once your passport is in their hands, that's it. They start requesting money for this and money for that—what should have cost only £50 ends up costing you around £1,000.

I eventually ended up with a visa, which they told me would allow me to travel to Malta, from where I would be issued with a transit visa to go to Bruges. My mother, my sisters, my nieces and nephews were all at the airport to wave me off. Everyone was so proud and so happy—I was embarking on my hopes and dreams. When we touched down in Malta I disembarked from the aeroplane and waited in line for a connecting flight to Belgium. But when it was my turn and I handed over my passport and visa the guy looked at it and laughed saying, 'I'm sorry, but this is a one-way student visa to Russia.'

I had little choice but to swap lines and board the flight to Russia. There was no way I could ask the plane to take me back to Cameroon, I had to finish the journey. I thought that there must have been some error and that I could sort it out once I had arrived in Moscow. I was very naïve. I arrived at Sheremetyevo International Airport in Moscow on May 1, 1997, six months shy of my eighteenth birthday. When the immigration officer asked my name in perfect English, I could not speak, my lips were frozen. I had never felt such cold in my entire life. My hand shook as I held out my passport. She must have laughed inside as she stamped my passport with a wry smile and said, 'Welcome to Russia,' in her mother tongue. The gates were opened and I entered Russia for the first time. What went through my mind was I was here in Russia but my mother and my family did not know where I was—they thought I was on my way to Bruges. I wasn't scared at that point, just shocked—I had swapped the frying pan for the fire. I never really got angry with the people who had done this to me for, at that time, I was still processing the venom I had inside for what my father's family had done to me—if death had embraced me in Russia, I would have accepted it without grumbling.

The biggest shock I had was that I was surrounded by black people – I had expected Russia to be full of white folks. What I didn't realise at the time was that we were all victims of human traffickers. In the arrivals hall I was met by a welcoming committee of thin-looking black men and women, with red eyes, like something out of a British Red Cross pamphlet, all waiting for their prey. It was easy. Most of the people at the airport were lost or stranded and presented easy pickings when it came to scamming money. The new arrivals had money and needed to be amongst people they knew. You would be approached, lied to and taken somewhere on the outskirts of Moscow. When your money was finished, you would be left to your own devices, abandoned. If the Russian skinheads didn't finish you off, the severe Russian weather would.

Among the parasites you could see the well-dressed puppet masters, the human trafficking barons, surveying the unfolding tragedy of dashed hopes and ruined lives.

I just stood in the midst of it all and tried to take in my predicament. 'Where do I begin? Where do I go? Where are the gods of my ancestors? Why has such a curse been placed upon my young shoulders?'

Looking at the problem today, governments are doing things to tackle the situation but it is worse now and in countries such as Cameroon people are still victims—people still want to leave their country and if someone knows that, then you are easy prey for human traffickers—more so if you are a woman. The only solution is to have an economic balance in the world, otherwise everybody is leaving and there are too many channels to be exploited. Like in Russia.

Sheremetyevo International Airport, located around eighteen miles north west of Moscow, was a long way from home and a scary place; not least to someone who had expected to find themselves entering Belgium. The various universities had arranged for their students to be picked up but I did not recognise anyone. Not a single soul. As I was getting lost in my thoughts, a well-dressed man approached me and introduced himself as Diamond.

'How much money have you got?' he asked.

'Money?' I thought to myself.

I reached into my pocket and brought out 3,000 CFA francs, the equivalent of three US dollars. He looked at me and said, 'Why are you carrying francs? It's of no use to you here, you need dollars.' He took the money from my hand and walked off towards another group of students. I later realised that we were being screened into the haves and the have-nots. The only thing that saved me was that from the very first day they realised that I was broke. I was useless. If I had been a woman, I would have been put to many uses.

I reached into my bag; my mother had prepared some of my favourite food, corn cookies and egusi pudding, but they were frozen solid, inedible. I felt like crying. I looked around – the sky was unfamiliar, the cold was biting into my bones and I could not see the earth's horizon. A shadow of despair began to descend but fortunately—or so I thought at that point—Diamond came back and said I could jump on the bus with them to central Moscow. However, he added quickly, from central Moscow, I would be on my own and should start making alternative travel arrangements.

Around half an hour later I found myself in the capital city of one of the last countries on this earth that I would wish to settle in. One of the first things I noticed was that all the pedestrians were walking so fast. Central Moscow was even colder than the airport, my small jacket and blue jeans, which were only suitable for the Cameroonian summer, had been eaten up by the cold. I felt like I was inside a freezer, it was torture. Even the little rays of sun that pierced through the skies felt cold. I thought of my mother and wondered what she would say if she knew where I was at that point in time—at the airport in Douala, she'd taken my hands into hers and, one by one, she gave each of my fingers a gentle bite. In doing so, she begged for both God and my ancestors to guide my path and return me home safely.

I was awoken from my reflections by the student liaison officer who was sent by Stavropol State University to meet Diamond. She was shouting at prospective students to hand their passports over to her so she could get their train tickets. As I wondered what I should do, Diamond approached and, despite previously warning me I would be one my own, offered to help me. I later realised it was all part of his elaborate scam. He told me the price of the ticket was twenty-five dollars and that he was going to get my ticket for me, however, as soon as I received my money from Cameroon, I was to reimburse the money back to his girlfriend, Agatha, who was also at the airport with us.

The old chestnut about 'money coming from home' was often one that I used, it got me out of a lot of problems but like many of my schemes, it eventually died an unnatural death. People's patience ran thin, others wanted advanced payment, and, of course, the money never came. However, with a promissory note to Diamond, I was allocated a space on the train with the other students and found myself headed for Stavropol.

Chapter 2

The train journey to Stavropol took four days, during which I made friends with a fellow Cameroonian called Rico, who told me his younger brother was already in Stavropol and was expecting him. Each time we stopped, old ladies would climb onto the train to sell food, which brought memories of similar such practice back home when Cameroon traders would jump on and sell everything from road kills to alligator eggs. Fortunately Rico made sure I had something to eat; we became good friends and the last I heard he was in Germany whilst his brother is now in France.

As the train lumbered along, I looked through the window at the snow, which, while starting to disappear, hung on in huge quantities on rooftops; it was the first time I had seen snow. My mind drifted to my brother who was a star history student and used to organise private classes for my friends. I would hear him talk at length about the Eastern Front, during the Second World War, and how the hostility of the Russian weather had crippled the German advances during operation Barbarossa. In my mind's eye I saw soldiers whose boots had been turned rotten by the snow; I saw starving faces and people eating dead horses; I saw women being raped; I saw soldiers whose legs had been eaten up by the snow.

'What was I doing in Russia?' I asked myself. 'Where was I going?'

*

I grew up in a small compound in the village of Wovilla, in the township of Buea, just under the foot of Mount Fako (Mount

Cameroon). The British Ambassador to Uzbekistan Craig Murray, in his book The Orangemen of the Congo, describes Cameroon as God's Gift to mankind—and he is correct, it's a beautiful country.

I am one of six children, well five children as one of my sisters died in the early part of 2000. Apart from my youngest sister, Queenta, whose father I met and knew, the rest of us were born either because of a one-night-stand or an illicit relationship my mother had with a married man. My mother tells me she loved my father.

My mother was the first of many children fathered by my grandfather, Mosre Mo Ngwa Kange (translated as the Dog of Dawn Kange) and was born out of wedlock. My grandfather proceeded to marry two other wives and fathered plenty of children. His compound was vast and he made his wealth working for the Colonial regime. He spent many years in Nigeria hence my mother is fluent in most Nigerian languages.

Until the last two months prior to my leaving Cameroon, my brother and I were not at all close. In fact, our relationship was so bad that he arranged for two of his friends to mug me. One evening, while walking home from town in darkness, I was grabbed by the legs and hands and my brother proceeded to beat me up mercilessly. The one thing that saved me was the fact that at the time I was large and carried a lot of weight, so difficult to contain, and my loud screams woke up many neighbours. In the confusion I managed to escape their clutches and ran off around the back of some houses, over a bridge and into my mother's house. My brother never came home that night.

The incident was reported to Chief Ben Morake and as punishment my brother and his cronies were ordered to buy three crates of alcohol for the village chiefs and were made to apologise to the whole village for their misdemeanours. You may think they got off lightly but I dished out some punishment of my own. A couple of days after the chiefs had enjoyed themselves with the gifts of repentance from my brother and his gang, using a catapult, I almost took out my brother's left eye. As if that was not enough, a couple of weeks later, I stabbed my brother's left arm with a fork.

9

'Wake up Eric!' Rico's voice brought me back from my reminiscences. The train had stopped in a small village and Agatha was giving the students a run down on Russian history. I could only understand one or two words, as her accent was very strong. Agatha looked like a man. She was of medium build with cropped hair and appeared to have no breasts, unless they were compressed beneath her clothes. She looked permanently angry and her demeanour reminded me of a strict nun.

There was a divide amongst the students travelling to Stavropol; the majority were not Cameroonians but Ibo Nigerians who had obtained Cameroonian passports through the black market. They were the ones fuelling this trade in human trafficking. Many of these Nigerians had ended up in a part of Cameroon called Kumba having been brought there as children and made to toil for a master day and night. In learning their trades, some of these guys became serious scammers and indulged in all kinds of illicit activities. In fact, my sister's husband fell prey to one such scammer. You see, he wanted a Suzuki motorcycle to be bought and transferred from Nigeria. Unfortunately he trusted and handed his hard-earned income to one of these Ibo boys. The guy took the money and was never seen again. The irony is that my brother-in-law was a seasoned customs officer in charge of stopping these cross-border activities between Cameroon and Nigeria. We later laughed about this incident but he was very sore when he realised he'd been scammed.

Yes, factions were showing amongst the travellers on the train. The English the Ibo guys spoke was so broken we could hardly understand them. The divide was amplified when the Ibo Nigerians decided to only speak in their Ibo language. I could understand a few things as my mother speaks fluent Ibo, along with Ibibio and Yoruba. As the train edged along at the pace of a snail, I was lost once more in my reverie.

I remember my little goat called Evenya'a Mboli; I loved that goat so much. I fed her and watched her grow into a proper mother. It was my responsibility to release her from the Ewing (a sleeping space for the goats and other small domestic animals) every day when I came home from school and I used to skip along with her. One afternoon, after arriving home from school, I released Evenya'a Mboli and a few minutes later I heard my uncle, Mola (Mola at the beginning of a name is a sign of respect, it means uncle) David, shouting, 'Eric! Come quick!' When I came out to meet my uncle, he looked distraught and said, 'Pa Takesh has killed Evenya'a Mboli!'

'What are you talking about?' I asked and followed my uncle to where my beautiful goat had been slain by a local hunter called Pa Takesh. I burst into tears for Evenya'a Mboli.

Pa Takesh had hunted all the little rodents in the village into extinction and had been eyeing up my goat, planning his fatal strike. As tradition demanded, I would be required to carry the carcass to the chief's compound to be divided between Pa Takesh, the villagers and me. I knew all this. I knew the villagers would be waiting for me. I went back home and got a big bowl, came back and bundled the remains of Evenya'a Mboli into it. As I did this, I discovered that she had been pregnant and that Pa Takesh's machete blow had sliced the kid goat in half.

I locked myself up in the kitchen and cried. Then I made a huge fire and burnt the hairs from the goat before cutting off pieces from the hind leg and roasting them on a banana leaf with some pepper and salt. Boy that goat tasted good. As I mourned, I ate and the tears made Evenya'a Mboli even tastier. I never took my goat to the elders. I vowed that if they wished to place a curse on my head, then so be it. Yes, they waited and all the while I was consuming bits of the goat. I never forgave Pa Takesh. Even when I heard he died, I only felt a small void because I never forgot he had killed my goat.

*

The first time I saw a trolley bus was when we arrived in Stavropol. We climbed on and the conductor smiled and said that we didn't need tickets. Unbeknown to us the Rector of Stavropol State University had taken out an advert in the *Stavropol Gazette* in an appeal to the people of the city to welcome new students. The goodwill from the locals continued until some AIDS test came back positive and the results were leaked to the public; overnight we went from being nice, exotic students from Africa to an abomination that needed purging.

Once on the university campus the students were allocated rooms inside Kulakova Hostel. From the top of the building you had a panoramic view of Stavropol, the birthplace of Mikhail Gorbachev, which is known as the Ring City as it is surrounded by trees.

The hostel had a communal kitchen, with a balcony that looked out directly towards the university, which was to prove a great vantage point to see if the university administrators were coming. If spotted, those of us who were not legitimate students would have enough time to climb the stairs all the way up to the 14th floor and hide. On arrival we had been asked to present our passports and I was given six months' residency, however, since I was not a registered student, I was not allowed to stay at the hostel. It became a cat and mouse situation between the authorities and me.

The Nigerians stayed to the right of the hostel and the Cameroonians to the left. I took refuge in what became known as the notorious room 11, which was home to those who could not pay their university fees, those who had lied about expecting money from their parents and those who did not know what time of the day it was. I was in the latter category. I had nothing; I ate when Rico and his brother ate—I also joined a prayer group, not by choice, but because after such meetings there would be food. Then someone stole my jacket, even though it wasn't suitable for the Russian winter. I later saw one of the Ibo Nigerians, a huge

12

chap, wearing it but I was terrified of approaching him, because his hands were as big as shovels.

Corruption was everywhere. A week after we arrived, the liaison officer appointed by the university to work alongside Agatha, mysteriously disappeared. He had collected money to the amount of fifteen thousand dollars from the students who could afford their fees. This guy had been studying medicine at Stavropol Medical Institute and was well trusted by the students. He was like a demigod due to the fact that he spoke fluent Russian. Little did the university, and the students, know he had bigger plans. By the time they realised what he was up to he was in St Petersburg and heading to Germany.

One heard all kinds of stories; there was one guy who'd been staying at the hostel long before we arrived, he hailed from a town in south west Cameroon called Mutengene, apparently, he had colluded with his friends and they had managed to obtain horse tranquillisers, which they used to sedate a businessman and stole all his money. He had exiled himself to Russia and was enjoying the money. He was rich and had a party every night.

As new arrivals in Stavropol, students or not, it was mandatory for us to take an AIDS test. We were arranged into small groups, blood was taken and a couple of days after the test, we had the results. I was clear and felt relieved, but a few others were not so fortunate, especially one couple I still remember, and one other girl. The girl mysteriously disappeared but the couple were carried into a police van and to this day I do not know of their fate.

Soon after arriving, news was brought to the hostel by some of the students, who attended Russian language classes, about celebrations at Lenin Square. Andy, Rico, a few Ibo guys, and myself decided to go to Lenin Square and join in the celebrations. It was beautiful, filled with beaming searchlights, looking as though they'd reached the heavens, and military parades, filled with everyone from young cadets to seasoned soldiers, marching in such harmonious rhythms.

I recalled one of my brother's lectures, on how the Russians celebrated Victory Day, and I was in the middle of it, watching history, albeit a reminiscence of it. I was in a state of complete trance, the marching soldiers, their songs, such pride for their country. A photographer asked if we would like our pictures taken as the soldiers marched by. This was my first picture taken in Russia; although a lack of money meant I never saw what it looked like.

On the return journey the trolley bus was packed. Rico was sat behind Andy and I, when two beautiful Russian girls got on the bus, and one of them approached and sat on my knees. My heart was pounding, Andy and Rico looked in shock, and other Nigerians looked agape. The Russian began touching my hair carefully, touching my jaw, she was saying something but none of us understood a single word; the other Russians around us laughed, mockingly, or so I thought. She talked all the way to the final stop, just across the road from Hostel Kulakova. I pointed towards the hostel gesturing it was where I lived. That night, all the guys thought I had brought juju (witchcraft—they thought I had charmed the girl) from my village.

The following morning, at around 11 a.m., there was a knock on room 11; when Andy opened it, the girl I had met the previous evening was there along with her friend. Everyone in room 11 was nervous or shocked. The students had been told not to trust the Russians, in fact, the university had explicitly told the students to avoid making friends with Russians. I had broken a golden rule. Fortunately the girl had brought a Russian English dictionary and after many attempts, I finally learned that her name was Helga. She and her friend had come to invite us to a picnic. The Cameroonians clamoured to advise me not to even think about it because it was a dangerous idea, me alone in the forest with a group of Russians. I pointed out the word 'food' and she shook her head saying, 'There is plenty of food.'

I managed to convince a boy known as Small Joe to accompany me—we had clicked as soon as we had met. Small Joe was kind, softly spoken and we would go around different rooms together and engage in empty conversations with their occupants until food was cooked, we would then share their food and return to room 11 to wait until our stomachs started rumbling again. I cried when a few months after arriving in Stavropol, Small Joe had to return to Cameroon as one of his brothers had died. Although I was wary, the thought of food spurred me on. We left through the back of the hostel and went deep into the woods. I had never been on a picnic—why would anyone want to go on picnic in my village? We have dangerous animals, including mambas, in the countryside. We arrived at the picnic area and joined a group of around twenty Russians and ate a combination of salad, roast lamb and some fruits I had never seen before. We also drank vodka and Pivo (beer). I was eating so much I'm sure Helga was concerned; she held the dictionary open and showed me the words African and starving. I laughed, we laughed. That was the best food I had eaten since I left Cameroon.

After the food, we played games and chased each other around. The last game we played was tug of war but, unfortunately, the rope snapped and Helga fell, banging her head on the hard ground; she was bleeding. I remember reading a novel called *Vendetta*, about seizing moments. This was my moment. I helped her sit upright and used some tissues to clean her up. Once the bleeding had stopped, we held hands and walked back towards the hostel. She hugged me and kissed me on the lips. We walked across the fields to her bus stop. It took me what felt like ten hours to reach the hostel that evening. That was the first time I kissed a white girl. I had forgotten about my plight; I could not sleep, I was thinking about Helga and her soft lips.

We spent the next couple of days together, Helga and I, whilst Small Joe was with Helga's friend. She was a bit concerned that I was not able to buy so much as a bottle of Coke. We went to a beautiful park; it was the first time I had been on a roller coaster ride. Helga was full of laughter all through whilst Small Joe and I were dying—in fact, I felt so poorly, I wanted to jump out. I promised myself never again. They laughed at us, she showed me the word 'derevnya', meaning village, implying I was a village boy. I said, 'Yes', and she promised never to take me on the rides again.

I had made some Russian friends that I met at the football fields. One of them, not much older than me, spoke a tiny bit of English. The first thing he advised me against was the way I used my hands expressly when talking. He said some people would misconstrue it as me being rude and it might get me into conflicts. I also met a guy who turned out to be one of the biggest mafia types in Stavropol. He had lent me one hundred and fifty dollars on the promise that I was travelling to Moscow to retrieve money sent to me by my father. When I could not afford to repay him, he and his humongous henchmen came and locked down the hostel for four hours. He promised to put my body parts on every bus stop in Stavropol if I did not give his money back. Fortunately for me an emergency collection was held in the hostel that came up with the money to bail me out; otherwise I would have been vaporised.

One Sunday Helga came to the hostel and said we should go for another picnic, only this time it would be just the two of us. I felt so excited. We crossed the fields and went into a shop not far from the hostel, where we bought some drinks. We found a clear patch and sat down and kissed. She removed my shirt and gradually I removed hers. Our lips never left each other's. I was thinking to myself, 'What would my brother make of this scenario?'

I had spent the last two weeks in Cameroon with my brother in his house in Douala; we spoke at length and patched up our differences—he then took me shopping and bought most of the clothes I wore to Russia. As I thought about my brother, out of the corner of my eye, I saw a hand reaching and grabbing Helga's handbag. I looked up and there was a little dude running away with it. I jumped to my feet and gave chase—he must have panicked at the sight of me, almost naked, chasing him through the woods. He dropped the bag but made away with Helga's purse. By the time, I got back Helga was fully clothed, and try as I might, I could not rekindle the mood and she insisted on going home.

As we walked across the fields towards the hostel, she was called over by one of the university's sports instructors. She spoke with him for a few minutes then, instead of coming towards me, Helga ran away. I was confused as to what that gentleman had said to Helga. I would soon guess, however, as when I came back to the hostel, I was shown a newspaper headline which said, 'African students have brought AIDS into Stavropol!' I never heard from Helga again.

Life moved on. We had discovered a bakery not far from the hostel and at the back of it was a small outhouse inside of which were kept tinned food. This became our food source for a few weeks until most of the students were taken ill; it was later discovered that the tinned food we had been consuming had long since passed its 'use by' date. They were stored in that outhouse to be used as feed for pigs.

*

I never knew hunger growing up as, on my way home from school, I would stop at my grandfather's compound where Mbombo (my grandfather's first wife) would have cooked Kwacoco and Mbanga soup. It is one of the delicacies of the Bakweri people that are readily available on all occasions from weddings to funerals. There was one old guy who attended funerals not because he knew the deceased but because of the aroma of Kwacoco, he always sat in the corner with his plate full, licking his fingers and crying at the same time. One could not decipher if he was crying for the deceased or the pure bliss from the food. It is even rumoured that the men of the Bakweri tribe ran away from military conscription because of this food, some men ran into the mountains to escape conscription but followed the smoke back into their mother's kitchen.

We would eat at Mbombo's kitchen, then move to Aunty Molisa's side of the compound where we would eat Vhembe (a kind of beans soup). Boy, Aunty Molisa was an expert at cooking Vhembe; it was either Vhembe or she also had another delicacy called Ngonya Weembe (a soup cooked using young coco yam leaves). Mbombo and aunty Molisa are both resting with my ancestors; I never said goodbye. I loved visiting my grandfather's compound not only because there was food at each of his wives' houses but because I was fascinated by his collection of old newspapers. I was an ardent reader of news, albeit posthumously.

It was in my grandfather's study that I first read about Kwame Nkrumah and Jerry Rawlings; it was here that I learned of the Congo Crisis of 1961 and the emergence of Colonel Joseph Mobutu of the Congolese National Army and how he had orchestrated a coup d'état and ordered the Soviets out of the country; it was here I first learned the phrase conspiracy theory as one newspaper article was suggesting that Britain and Belgium conspired to murder the second United Nations Secretary General, Dag Hammarskjold, as both countries had a vested interest in keeping the rich diamonds and Copperfield of Zaire under their sphere of influence. It was here that I researched and attempted to answer the history question at A-levels, 'The Arab-Israeli question is a hard nut to crack, discuss.' It was here that I first read about the great Thomas Sankara, it was here that I learned of the whereabouts of President Ahmadou Ahidjo, whose corpse was abandoned in Senegal somewhere, and how Mr Biya has been the president since 1982. It was here that I read about South Africa and the Afrikaans Medium Decree of 1974, it was here that I learned about The Sharpeville Massacre in South Africa of 21 March 1960. For a long time I hated white South Africa. It was here that I read about Steve Biko and the imprisonment of Nelson Mandela—it all sounded so fictitious and farfetched, for how can a visitor come and impose such draconian, inhumane policies upon the natives? I was naïve.

It was here in my grandfather's study that I first heard about Winnie Mandela, the exile of Lucky Dube and the beautiful voice of

Miriam Makeba, and, most importantly, it was here that I learned and read at length about the Rwandan genocide. After being accused of witchcraft my grandfather was abandoned by his family, but I only have fond memories of him. The last time I visited before I left Cameroon he said, 'Ngalle come here.' Holding a bowl of water, my grandfather washed my hands, my feet, and my face and performed what we call a zromelelele, an invitation and incantation to the gods of my ancestors. He called on the god of heaven to protect me as I crossed many seas, oceans and mountains. He said I should be aware of the various ndondondume (a mythical beast that lures humans into catastrophic demise) that would try and entice me with the beautiful things in life. Then he bid me farewell and a safe journey. I would never attest to what others have said about the late Mosre Mo Ngwa Kange being a witch, for if he was truly a witch, this would have been his perfect time to initiate me.

*

I was always outside the hostel grounds. It was getting warmer and I was making some Russian friends, most of whom were interested in teaching me the Russian language. At other times we played football with a local Armenian team, most of them being students at the university. One of the Armenians, a guy called Aaron, visited the hostel and told us about a city called Sochi. It was on the coast and he said that he owned several yachts and that he could take us for excursions to Turkey and back via the Black Sea. This caused great excitement in the hostel and I thought, 'This is my perfect opportunity to leave Russia.'

In order to confirm that Aaron indeed had a yacht in Sochi, a delegation was formed to investigate and three Ibo Nigerians and I were to travel to Sochi on a fact-finding mission. One of the Nigerians was the huge-handed chap who had stolen my jacket; he even wore it during our trip to Sochi.

Travelling the near five hundred miles from Stavropol to Sochi was an eight-hour drive by bus; I could understand why people preferred to stay in the same place. Despite the arduous journey our first trip to Sochi proved futile; yes there was a yacht club and we could go to Turkey, as often as we would have wanted but there was one slight problem—in order to leave Russia, we needed an exit visa.

There was worse to come as on our way back to Stavropol we missed our train. We jumped onto another train but went via a town called Mineralnye Vody, and after getting off to stretch our legs, we found ourselves stranded in this town. I heard the sound of harsh voices shouting, 'Stop! Hands in the air!' I turned around to see some Russian soldiers—I had never seen such humongous men. Their faces were covered with black cloth and they didn't wear helmets but some military style khaki caps. My large Nigerian companion began crying and I thought, 'That's what you get for stealing my jacket.'

The soldier in front of me had his gun pointed directly at my head. I had tremendous flashbacks. I started seeing the faces of my father's family members, specifically those who had attended the court on the final day of the hearing with regards to my father's estate. I started seeing the villagers, especially the local town crier and tramp from Longstreet who had placed herself in front of us and had broken the news to the entire village. I saw those women who pointed fingers and mocked my mother.

*

To this day, I have not seen a picture of my father. I love my name 'Ngalle', because it is the one thing I have that attaches me to my late father, for 'Eric' and 'Charles' are colonial implants. I used to go through the collection of photographs in my aunt's house, but there was not a single picture of my father. When I visited the printing press where my father had worked, his belongings had been given to my adopted sister but his photographs had disappeared; in fact, my father's job was handed to my adopted sister upon his death.

20

My mother would always point and show me the window from whence my father first spotted her—I promise I will write about this window one day, the window from where the gods congregated and planned my fallopian explosion into my first exile; the window from whence my father whispered to the winds, who took their turns in whispering to the trees, who carried his whispers into my mother's kitchen and into her ears. Every time my mother went past this window, she stood and stared—she too was once in love. I could tell and I would ask, 'Did you love my father?' She would smile wryly and slap me gently on the back of the head.

I dread to think my father's family had been planning to erase his memory from me and, in so doing, erase him effectively. I sincerely dread this prospect. My father's name never came up in any conversations, I was just the child of a loose woman who had been condemned and found guilty by the villagers and my paternal kinsmen.

*

I wanted to go back to Cameroon; Russia was a stranger to me. I was going to lay my father's compound in ruins and anything or anyone that was inside. I couldn't care less, I was ready to lobotomise that part of my brain that thought of Wonya Morake or Oscar or Ngalle. These are the perfect laid plans I was nursing in my mind until I arrived in Moscow. As the gun got closer to me, I prayed although my faith in God was dwindling. I pleaded and asked God and Satan, (both had possessed me) that even if I were to die that day, my spirit would return to Cameroon and forever wreak havoc on those who had done this damage to me, as here I was, about to be shot dead in a foreign field. I hated my village, I hated my father and, more so, I hated his family.

The soldiers kept shouting—they must have thought we were terrorists who had sworn allegiance to the gods of a voiceless clan. We didn't have a clue what they were shouting about but we knew that we were in immediate danger.

It transpired that we had managed to find ourselves in the middle of a war zone, between Russia and Chechnya, and we were considered to be Chechen dissidents. We were handcuffed, bundled into four different Land Rovers and driven off to a police station. We were locked in different cells with our handcuffs left on. After a few hours, we were taken into a room with four chairs and were interviewed at length by the Chief Inspector; she was stunningly beautiful. Mercifully, she soon established that we were residents of Stavropol and not Chechen rebels. She resorted to speaking in the most perfect English and explained to us that Mineralnye Vody was a buffer zone between Russia and Chechnya. She warned us about the dangers of roaming the area, without an appropriate guide, and spoke about the Chechen war at length. She then gave us tea, sardines, bread and cheese.

Once we had finished eating, she called some plain clothes officers who proceeded to accompany us to the train station and waited for us to get on the train. We arrived back in Stavropol without further mishap. That night, I missed my mother. I ventured out onto the hostel's balcony and prayed—I even poured tea onto the ground, a tradition we always did back home, calling upon my ancestors to come and fly me home; they never did, maybe because I had used a non-alcoholic drink. I felt very homesick; even the Russian skies were alien to me. There was nothing familiar.

Chapter 3

Returning to Sochi

Although the AIDS headline in the newspaper had caused us much derision, our reputation as black exotic students was to be restored by the visit of the pop group Boney M. to Stavropol. As I was not a student, I was not restricted by the guidelines imposed by the university, which declared, 'You should not make friends with Russians.' In fact I did not have a choice. I had to roam; I had to look for greener pastures. In so doing I was making friends and acquaintances.

One such friend was Vladimir who, I was quite excited to discover, spoke English. Vladimir had a receding hairline and was dressed like a pimp; everything about him was shiny. He was an extrovert indeed, he smiled a lot and, for the duration of time I knew him, he was never angry. He had come up with the idea of starting a Black Dance and Arts Class in Stavropol and decided that the best place to recruit members was our hostel.

One afternoon Vladimir came to the hostel with two tickets for a concert at the Dynamo Stavropol Stadium and a fellow Cameroonian and I were the lucky ones to be at home in room 11 that afternoon.

These were not just any tickets, they were front row tickets, and they gave us backstage access as well. The stadium itself was packed, full capacity. We danced to all their songs—including 'Ra Ra Rasputin'—and a young black guy with them was performing all sorts of acrobatics on-stage. We forgot all about our woes and got up and danced. Then Boney M. spotted us and they moved in our direction and the whole crowd cheered.

23

It got even better as Chris and I accepted their invitation to join them on stage. This was heaven for us. We had never been to a music concert before, let alone one of such magnitude. The whole of the stadium waved as we danced. Boney M. looked like they'd come from another planet, they were black, I mean American black—it was like they'd use coco butter on their skin whilst we had been using coco soap. They looked perfect, majestic.

After the concert, they took us to their hotel. We ate like people who had been deprived of food. Vladimir must have told them we were on the verge of starvation as they passed all their food to us. From shrimps to caviar to fish soup, it all came our way. We had a camera from somewhere and took lots of photographs or selfies, as you would call them today. If only there had been Instagram back then we would have been trending.

We became famous again in Stavropol; momentarily people had forgotten about their AIDS concerns. People would wave to us on the streets, thinking we were part of the Boney M. clan. After a couple of weeks, the novelty had passed and people started noticing that our black skin was not as perfect as that of Boney M. First the ticket controllers were hot on our case and secondly, when we were on the bus, most people just moved away. We became like the plague again.

It was during this time that a small selection of Cameroonians decided that I should go back to Sochi and explore the possibility of travelling to Istanbul once more. While I knew there was no way we would be able to cross Russian waters into Turkey without an exit visa, I encouraged them to try. My thinking was that if I could manage to get the students to Sochi, I could concoct a scam of my own and charge inflated prices, which would give me enough money to vamoose to Moscow and arrange for my repatriation to Cameroon. So I made my way to the coast once more.

When you arrive in Sochi you are greeted by the beautiful sight of a fleet of boats, yachts and warships on the water and on a perfect summer's day one can see across to Ukraine. My journey was smooth; I slept on the train and arrived in Sochi first thing in the morning. I caught a taxi to Zhemchuzhina Grand Hotel, the same place we had stayed during our first visit, and discovered music blasting from the seafront.

I decided to explore and was surprised as I walked along the beach, that a lot of people approached and took pictures with me. Some of them shouted 'Black monkey!' and I laughed as they mocked me. I loved the attention and it was water off a duck's back to me.

I saw a tanned white guy on a boat who beckoned me over and offered me some vodka and pomidory (tomato). I climbed on-board and he asked about the reason for my visit to Sochi. We spoke for a while and then he took me for a twenty-minute sail during which I made my pitch. It was the same thing, they could take us to Istanbul for a fee of three hundred dollars per head, however, we needed those exit visas.

When I returned to the hotel, I communicated this to the students in Stavropol, but I had inflated the price from three to four hundred dollars. I also insisted that we did not need exit visas. This was a big, fat lie. It wasn't a surprise when a mysterious courier conveyed to the students what my master plans were—the Ibo Nigerians who were part of our first visit to Sochi had grassed me up.

I sat back and waited for the students to arrive but they never turned up. On the fifth day, when I phoned the hostel, there was no answer. Panic kicked in. I had gone two days without making payment at the hotel; once again I had told the management that my friends were coming with money to cover the hotel bills. I spent most of the evenings sat on the benches outside the hotel with dreams floating back and forth between my village and where I now was. On one evening a Russian woman came and sat next to me. She had a *Playboy* magazine and together we perused the pages. Before I knew it, she was kissing me. We soon disappeared

25

into my hotel room and we had sex. Afterwards I smoked my first ever cigarette. My bliss was soon dispelled when I was summoned to the hotel security lodge and told I had until Sunday to pay for my accommodation, or my passport would be handed to Sochi immigration.

Then I met Froy. 'Excuse me, are you a born-again Christian?' This was the opening line of conversation between Froy and me. This was a very strange question; little did I know that Froy was an angel. I was brought up a Roman Catholic with very strict morals; in fact, after my A-levels, I had joined the Apostolic movement and followed them around as they did vigils in different villages.

'Are you familiar with the book of Daniel?' Froy asked, handing me a bible.

He then enquired about my accommodation arrangements before saying, 'My mother and I have rooms at our house; we rent them out in the summer to families who come to visit the Black Sea. We charge cheaper rents than the hotels. If you wanted to, I could pick you up from the hotel car park tomorrow and you could stay with us?'

This was divine intervention; I could not say no. I told Froy that old lie, 'My parents will be sending me some money shortly.'

*

I was used to being shifted around. Once my mother had gone off with her friends, as they used to help each other in communal farming, and I was left at home with my nephew, Collins, and my younger sister, Queenta. Once, after I became hungry, I abandoned my sister and cousin and walked all the way to my grandfather's compound, which was around an hour and a half away, to report my mother missing. My grandfather, being the chief, summoned all the villagers and went off to search for my mother. When they arrived at our house in Tole, my mother was in the kitchen cooking. She was shocked; she had to buy three crates of beer for the elders and cook extra food for those who had gone to search for her.

A couple of weeks after this incident, my mother was involved in a car accident—she was knocked over and the wheels went over her stomach. She would have died if we had stayed at the Buea General Hospital, which served our village of Small Sappo. My mother was in so much pain but thanks to the insistence of my elder sisters, Elizabeth and Ndinge, she was rushed to a private hospital in Tiko, where they stopped her internal bleeding. I never left my mother's bedside.

When she felt better and we had returned home, I was summoned into the kitchen and told that I had to go and live with my sister, as it was my fault she'd been knocked over. Her theory was, I had angered the villagers by making them go on a search for her, and the villagers had placed a curse on her and the accident came to be. So, you see, I am used to being exiled.

*

The next day I packed my meagre belongings into my bag and I left the hotel. I did not pay the bill, the guards did not chase me, they simply handed my passport over to the Sochi Immigration Service, which was located not very far from one of the piers overlooking the Black Sea. Froy picked me up and that was the first time I saw a disabled person drive a car—Froy was dysfunctional from his waist down but had an extremely strong upper body.

We had a disabled guy in my village, he was a brother to everyone and we would all help to push him in his wheelchair but I could never imagine a scenario where he drove. I was shocked when Froy showed me his specialised Lada car. Froy spoke with so much passion and had an enthusiasm for life that was contagious.

27

Chapter 4

After settling in my new lodgings, Froy turned to me and said, 'Well Eric, for a fee of one hundred dollars a month, I will teach you how to speak Russian and show you around Sochi and introduce you to my friends at our Presbyterian Church.' That was my agreement with the Vladimirs. Every day after breakfast and his morning exercises, Froy dedicated two hours of his time towards teaching me the Russian language. Froy was patient and a very good teacher. We finished each lesson with an assignment for which I had plenty of help thanks to Tyotia, a ninety-seven-year-old babushka (babushka means old woman or grandmother), who lived opposite the Vladimirs. I cried when Tyotia died.

One of the first things Froy and I did was to go for a swim in the Black Sea. I made him laugh by asking if there were any crocodiles in the water. He remarked, 'You are a bushman, aren't you?' We both laughed.

*

When I was a boy, I had tried swimming to no avail; I even tried gymnastics but I failed at that too. I remember once, during one of the village's 20th May celebrations—our National Holiday after a referendum in 1972 to become a unitary country—being paired with another boy who was even fatter than I was. We were to do a chained cartwheel; the combination of our blubber shook the ground as we rolled. People shouted and clapped—we thought they clapped because we were good, not knowing that as we were rolling, we took out anything and everyone that was in our path. Those were the days. I was even worse at swimming.

Froy could swim. There were long concrete slabs, which reached far out into the sea, that you could run along and dive off performing all kinds of acrobatics. Some people even swam as far as the boats that could be seen on the horizon.

Slowly but steadily Froy taught me how to swim and how to speak the Russian language. He also introduced me to the Presbyterian faith.

I had used their house telephone to contact my maternal uncles in America. My mother has three brothers in America who are all citizens and one of whom, Uncle Evella, is a doctor and also in line to be the chief of my village. She explained that I was in terrible circumstances and needed around a thousand dollars. Froy was with me when I made this telephone call and heard the promises from my uncles that they would send me some money. The money never came. My uncles reassured my mother that they'd sent me some financial assistance, but this was not the case. Still, I am grateful they told white lies to my mother.

Froy also introduced me to a guy known as Anthony who was a small-time mafia guy. Anthony and his friend Aaron, an Armenian who owned a small garage just outside the city centre, were to be very kind to me. Somehow the immigration officials in Sochi had tracked me down and visited the Vladimir's household. Fortunately Anthony and Aaron came up with the two hundred dollars I owed the hotel and paid a total of two hundred and fifty dollars to retrieve my passport. However, I was told very strongly that I was not a resident of Sochi, I had no reason to be there, and I was illegal. I was only legally allowed to stay in Stavropol but that privilege too was expiring in a matter of months.

Tania, Froy's mother, was in her early fifties and unhappy; you could see this by the extra wrinkles that appeared on her face every morning. Her husband spent most of his summer at their dacha (a holiday home). If you met Tania, you would know that she must have been an absolute beauty when she was younger; she was tall, elegant and had those extra-long legs, which suited her career choice: dancer and ballerina.

She invited me several times to see her performing and to watch the Sochi Symphony Orchestra. Tania was unhappy that since my stay in their family home, I had not made any monetary contributions into the family coffers. No one knew how to help me; I didn't know how to help me. Despite all this, Tania took pity on me and treated me like her own child; I was falling in love with the family, the more I did so the more I hated my paternal family. I cursed them.

Then one September evening, Anthony and his friend Aaron, smuggled me out of Griboedova to a small Armenian village—where Aaron lived—on the lands that gradually stretch up to form Mount Akhun. I had picked up a great deal of the Russian language by this time and Anthony had invited me to a family wedding. The wedding was a feast. The whole table was full of food from top to bottom—it reminded me of a scene in Chinua Achebe's *Things Fall Apart* where the food was piled so high that only after it had been consumed did visitors realise their family members were on the other side of the table.

I couldn't help but notice a rather attractive girl who I later learned was called Natalia. It turned out she was quite taken by me as although she was sat next to Anthony, she had insisted they changed places so she was right next to me. She offered me some of her chicken drumsticks and told me she'd been to America and really loved black Americans. This was my cue. I told her I was an African American and showed her the pictures of Lisa from Boney M. and told her that she was my mother.

She looked at the pictures with intense curiosity and, after a few minutes, she tapped me on the shoulder and as I turned around our lips met in a proper kiss.

The party was in full swing. The bride was showered with gifts, an Armenian band was playing, Anthony and Aaron danced with their shirts unbuttoned, in unison with their family members, vodka flowed and there was merriment galore. Then among the guests I saw the face of Chief Justice Paul and heard him ask the question, *'Do you know that boy Eric Ngalle Charles? Do you know him?'* I could see hollow faces and their response ricocheting like the voice of a missing mountaineer. I could feel some tears and pretended to sneeze. I appeared to be welcomed around the village and my visit rolled into a stay of several weeks.

'Who is this?' It was Natalia's mother asking her who I was.

'It's Eric, my friend,' replied Natalia. I was invited to their home, a two-storey building with a huge garden growing all kinds of fruit, especially grapefruits and passion fruits. Natalia and I played Adam and Eve, for truly, this was our Eden.

Every day on his way to work, Aaron would drop me at the library, which was owned by Natalia's family. I was a local celebrity. A tourist attraction. I would tell the children stories about Ndondondume (a mythical beast from Bakweri mythology, who lures his victims with an amazing singing voice before devouring them) and when my Russian was not enough, Natalia translated.

*

I was a master storyteller and my favourite story was about Yomadene, a mythical beast that lives on top of Mount Cameroon. I also loved the story of Epassamoto, a half-stone, half-human who took care of Albino children abandoned to die on top of the mountain— when I was growing up, there were two Albino twins in our village and I was always terrified for their fate. I also loved the mystics of the Ekulelekule or tortoise.

Years later I told my daughter these stories as we looked through the window of our housing association accommodation in Ely, Cardiff, overlooking the city centre; the Millennium stadium, smoke from Brains Brewery and the roof tops of Splott and Broadway. I would tell my daughter all these beautiful stories but she would still be pointing at Eric Carle's book The Very Hungry Caterpillar—*it was her favourite book. I guess it was her way of telling me I had completed my metamorphosis now that I had met her. It was as if the spirits of my ancestors had conveyed to her, mysteriously even before she was born, that I was coming all the way from my village in Cameroon via the mountains of Akhun in Sochi Russia, to be her father on a council estate called Ely in a small corner of Wales.*

*

We did not have any breathing space, even when we hid behind the library shelves to kiss; there was always one babushka that wanted to ask if I had met Nelson Mandela.

At times, to entertain them, I used to play some African drums. The villagers loved me; Natalia and her parents loved me. I spent most nights at Natalia's home, although we never slept in the same room. I used to help Aaron's father cut the grass in the garden, prepared their bunker and kept the winter fruits in jars and all kinds of containers. It was a village, I was a village boy, and I loved it.

Towards the end of my stay I was invited on an excursion. We drove with a few other acquaintances deep into the foothills of Mount Akhun—if Anthony and Aaron had bad plans for me this would be their big chance; the road was very narrow, I could have been pushed over a huge drop and no one would have been any the wiser. You see, I had been living on the kindness of strangers— I had three meals a day, not just any meals, proper cooked meals—but I had started to sense I was beginning to overstay my welcome. The money that I had said was coming was not forthcoming. It reached the point where they would ask me to dial my family in America; I would miss a digit on purpose.

The car finally stopped at the foot of Mount Akhun and we got out. To my relief a picnic was unfolded and we jumped into a welcoming waterfall. At first, I was apprehensive and when, once again, I asked if there were any crocodiles, Anthony burst out laughing. This was a running joke: every time we met, he would remind me about crocodiles in Russia.

Days passed. Despite my fears being unfounded I knew I was not going to receive money from anyone and I could not carry on with that old lie about me waiting for money. On top of this Aaron told me that the immigration officers had stopped him and said that they knew he was harbouring an illegal immigrant and that I had to leave Sochi.

At the same time, I was summoned to Natalia's house. Natalia had applied for a visa and was accepted to come to the United Kingdom as an au pair but she had locked herself in her room insisting she would only go if her parents ensured I travelled with her. There was no way this was going to happen. We all had to compromise. My passport was photocopied and with Anthony as a witness, Natalia and I were married traditionally in front of her mother and father, brother, nieces and nephews.

To this day I am not sure about the legality of this marriage; it was just done to pacify Natalia. It wasn't a full-on wedding, as firstly, the authorities would have told the family I was not American, secondly, I was illegal and would not have been allowed to marry Natalia if things were done properly. I miss Natalia very much and I hope one day we meet again. In fact, I cry secret tears for her most nights. Three days later Natalia travelled to the UK.

Chapter 5

Eventually, I had overstayed my welcome. I did not have any money yet strangers who had their own families to take care of were feeding me. I had become an unnecessary burden. Though Anthony and Aaron never directly told me, I could tell our friendship was strained, their excitement of having a black boy around was fading and fading fast, so they took me to Sochi main bus station and I boarded a bus back to Stavropol. Natalia's parents filled my bags with all kinds of fruits from their garden. They also gave me their house telephone number and Natalia's telephone number in York.

When I returned to Stavropol I discovered that Andy and Rico, who had been the first people I had made friends with on my arrival in Russia, had left after deciding to take their chances of making it to Europe via Ukraine, while Small Joe was on his way to Moscow to return to Cameroon; he'd lost his younger brother and his parents had bought him an air ticket and the university issued him with an exit visa. There was also some anger brewing towards me back at the hostel as, not long after my return, Anthony and his friends had been intimidating the students and enquiring as to my whereabouts. He wanted the money he had paid out for my passport and hotel fees. He had already confused Chris for me at one of the bus stops and his friends had pounced on him. On top of hiding from Anthony and his friends, the university authorities had increased their daily visits to the hostel, so I had to be extra careful. And then there was the cold to contend with.

The Russian winter of 1997 was one of the harshest on record and we would hear news stories of dedushkas (grandfathers) dying in the snow after consuming homemade vodka. I went along to a church session one evening, overseen by a self-proclaimed pastor. When he first came to the hostel, he was blacker than a Chadian soldier, however he began using one of those bleaching soaps; his face was as yellow as the sun and covered with pimples but his hands were blacker than roast plantains. He said he had a skin condition but everyone in the hostel knew he was using coco soap.

As we sat in the kitchen waiting for food (there was always food after a church session; God was kind to the illegals) Anthony and his friends walked in and dragged me out onto the balcony. I was suspended over the parapet—by this time I was as skinny as a stick insect. They proceeded to punch me in the ribs while Anthony, who looked rough and smelled of alcohol, shouted, 'Where's my money? Give me my money. I will fuck your mother and I'm going to fucking kill you.'

Normally when we made a loud noise the guard downstairs would rush up, but no one came on this occasion; perhaps they had been paid off. After what seemed like a lifetime, the hostel rallied and came up with the two hundred dollars—Anthony and his friends added fifty dollars in interest—and I was dragged back into the kitchen.

A few weeks after this incident, there was another attack, this time it wasn't by Anthony or his entourage, but the guards downstairs after one of them had been angered by one of the Ibo Nigerians who had shouted, 'Fuck your mother.' There was a small confrontation that was soon quelled by the university authorities, however the guards went away and planned their revenge. It was mid-December and the snow was thick. Suddenly we heard loud noises coming from the Nigerian side of the hostel. Two of our number, Saul and Chris, went out to investigate. Chris didn't return. His head was bashed in with a baseball bat. The guards had broken into the rooms and people were being battered.

Saul shouted, 'You guys should run, they've killed Chris.' The stairs were blocked and the only safe passage out was via the kitchen. Saul had already jumped into the snow from the third floor, in bare feet, and I quickly followed him, along with a few others who had managed to push the guards out of the way.

We ran onto the main road and flagged a taxi down, climbed in and asked the driver to take us to the nearest police station. He drove to the edge of town and abandoned us. There was no police station; it turned out the taxi was part of the assault team. Saul started crying, it was extremely cold and he was bare footed. It had gone past midnight and the trolley bus had stopped working. We managed to flag another taxi down and, fortunately, this time we were taken to the police station—if only we had studied our university environment, we would have known the police station was just across the road from the university.

The police appeared shocked by how fluent I was in the Russian language. I explained to the officer on duty that there was an attack taking place on the campus and within a few minutes the reception was full of huge police officers in riot gear carrying Kalashnikov rifles. By the time we got to the hostel, the siege had ended and there was blood all over the floor. The police officers had arrested most of the guards and some had been beaten. Chris and Grand Dan had suffered the worse beatings. Saul was carried to an ambulance and taken to hospital.

I offered to be the spokesperson, to represent the students against the university in the following inquest but was told, 'Eric, you are not a student, you will not be able to represent us.'

I didn't protest; I had my own plans. Whilst the crisis meeting took place, I went to the university canteen and used the phone. I called the rector pretending I was calling from the Cameroonian Embassy. 'Good afternoon, can I speak with the rector of the university please? My name is Patrice Ebutu and I am calling from the United Nations. We are deeply angry with what we are hearing from your university; we want action taken against the perpetrators.'

I was told that after this call the rector went into panic mode. The perpetrators held at the police station were charged with assault and their jobs at the university were under threat—being kicked out of the university meant going straight into the army. I made several such calls to the rector during this period but on the last occasion, having taken advantage of an empty canteen to use the telephone, a different voice answered; his secretary. Nina was a softly spoken girl with long, blonde hair and blue eyes, who spoke English with an American accent. All the students fancied her and I was no exception.

She started asking me about my role at the United Nations: was I attached to the Human Rights Commission? How long had I been working at the United Nations? She then said, 'The rector is busy but he won't be long, he knows you are on the line.' I was lost in the beauty of her voice and didn't notice two security officers creep up on me. I turned around and the rector gave me a serious slap. I was dragged outside the front entrance of the hostel and given a good beating. The Russian students were shocked. I couldn't fight back but I struggled and freed myself from their grip and ran towards the hostel. It turned out that the same shovel-hands Ibo Nigerian, who had stolen my jacket, had learned that I was the one making the telephone calls and had gone and grassed me up to the university authorities.

At this point my reputation was enhanced among the students. I was the most illegal of all. I had not set foot in any Russian language classes yet I spoke the language with such fluency it appeared to be my own. The university heavily compensated Chris and Dan. My one last heroic involvement in this matter was when Dan was again threatened at gunpoint in the reception area. He was being forced by the brother of one of the Russians who had been identified as the mastermind behind the attacks at the hostel to drop the case against his brother.

All the elders amongst the students were there and I had heard what was being said as I approached the noise. I addressed the guy with the gun by saying, 'Respected gentlemen. Let us not fight as if we were noise makers in a market.'

I had played the language to perfection. I had respected the guy and at the same time used slang that was rare and only used by one who had a mastery of street talk. The guy relaxed, looked at me and placed the gun in his bag before coming over and shaking my hand. He congratulated me on my language skills and enquired how long I had been at the hostel. I arranged a private meeting for the next day between the gentleman and Dan, in which Dan was well compensated and, for my negotiations, I was given one hundred dollars. No case was brought against anyone and we never had any problems again—until the four horsemen of the apocalypse arrived from Moscow telling us about buying and selling fake dollars that is. More on that later.

Hearing my sister's voice was always such a relief to me. She told me that my mother was well pleased that her brothers in American had sent me two thousand dollars. I laughed. I could not contradict her. She told me about her job, she was now working at the Prime Minister's office. Ndinge was trained as a skilled marksman, a sharp shooter and worked as a gendarme, a French paramilitary officer, she was so good she worked alongside the Former Prime Minister of Cameroon—who is currently languishing in Kondengui (a notorious prison) accused of corruption.

My sister told me about her two children, Aloga and Iya, and also about how the family in Cameroon had raised one million CFA francs, the equivalent of £1,500, which had been given to my nephew's father to send to me. The money never came and I am unable to confront him as to what happened to the money, as he died.

I told my sister I had to leave Russia, she promised to do all she could. I asked about my mother's farm; the last thing I did for my mother before embarking on this journey was to develop a nice yam plantation for her.

*

My mother and I have this strong bond, you see, as I stayed in her stomach for almost twelve months; she keeps reminding me of this. I think she must have got her dates of conception wrong, she even told me that I already had a tooth when I was born. In fact, I hated breast milk and would not stop crying at the hospital, until they brought me mashed potatoes. She might be telling the truth, who knows, but after me, no other child in the village has been named Eric. I remember when my brother had his first son, I begged for him to name the child after me, but he looked at me as if I had developed witchcraft; I was truly a cursed child.

*

It wasn't because we had never experienced winter before; it was because the winter of 1997 in Russia was just extraordinarily cold and extremely hostile. In my village, during the rainy season, people become very selective when it came to showering; we have a name for it, 'seba', you wash those parts of the body that are prone to smell. In Russia, we went for weeks without a shower. Don't get me wrong, the university ensured the hostel had plenty of heating and hot water, but it was just easier not to shower. It wasn't all bad though. The extreme winter had brought an opening in the job market and several of us got jobs as petrol station attendants. It paid well but there was no employment contract or anything like that; you relied on tips from generous customers who did not want to get out of their warm cars into the freezing cold.

Around this time Big Joe, Chris, who was just about recovered from his head injury, and I formed a small performing arts group; we were managed by a small guy called Maxim. We did around twenty concerts with the highlight being performing in front of the Mayor of Stavropol. Afterwards he invited us backstage but Maxim had told me that he was fond of boys so we made our apologies and exited the building.

We performed in several places including schools, we almost

started a riot in one, when the students realised that we were miming the hip pop artist Tupac, and they chased us off stage.

As the concerts were few and far between, Chris and I got a job working as DJs at a nightclub in Prospekt Mira, which was around twenty minutes from Kulakova where our hostel was located. The club was owned by a guy from Georgia called Baku and he paid us a hundred roubles a night; we worked Wednesday, Friday and Saturday. Unfortunately, the role was short-lived as far as I was concerned because a fatwa had been issued on me. You see, one night, after finishing my session at the club, I met this beautiful woman, called Nadia, and we spent the night at her house. The affair carried on for a couple of weeks, until I found out that she was married. The husband owned another nightclub so he was never home.

I only found out she was married when we kissed on a small bench outside her house and her husband came out to smoke a cigarette with his friend.

'Fuck your black arse!' he shouted, 'I will fucking kill you!'

I ran all the way back to the hostel. The following day, Nadia came to the hostel and begged me to sleep with her one final time. The hostel was shocked, thinking I had some sort of special charm with the ladies. The following Saturday I didn't go to work, as I was worried Nadia's husband would carry out his threat. Chris went alone but returned half hour later to say the police had cordoned off the nightclub—it turned out the owner had shot and killed his girlfriend. Chris was traumatised.

Around this time I became involved in a relationship with another Russian girl called Lola. We had been dating for a couple of months and I spent most evenings at her house after work. Lola was an only child, she had plans and ambitions to take over the world; we would spend the time weaving our dreams together.

We met when she had visited the hostel as part of a group of three girls, one of who started dating my friend Chris; they eventually left for Krasnodar together. Lola was a school dropout and spent most of her time visiting her friends and, I am sure, smoking weed.

At the time, I was also dating Agatha: she had joined our band, but she could not dance to save her life. Agatha was the first girl who gave me her home telephone number. I would call her in the evening using the telephone in the security office downstairs and we would spend an age talking.

One evening Lola came to the hostel crying; she had been told she was pregnant. She told me she wanted to keep the baby. Jejayeee! I didn't know what to say or how to advise her. In the end she followed her mother's advice and had an abortion. Later I moved out of the hostel, after making friends with a Cameroonian called James, and shared a flat with him on the sixth floor of a tall residential block in a nice community area; behind our house you could see the main motorway out of Stavropol. By now my stay in Stavropol had officially expired but I managed to doctor my documents and extended my residency permit; I had effectively issued myself with another six months stay. I got a job working at a petrol company owned by Lukoil; the boss was called Stanislav, which we shortened to 'Stars'. He was a young man and drove an Audi. We conversed in Russian and English.

Stars showed me pictures of his beautiful wife and his son. After our first shift, he invited me to his house and made one of my favourite dishes, gariatchi hachapuri, which is some sort of meat pie, more meat than pie, and is addictive. At this time I entered into a relationship with a Russian girl called Anna who ran a small bread kiosk near to where I lived. We later lived together and Anna almost became my wife although she would probably kill me now if she saw me—I left her with a broken heart. One day I was with her and the next I had disappeared.

There's a picture of Anna and I in my sister's house in Tiko Cameroon. I looked fresh and I sent it to Tiko just so my mum could see that I wasn't at death's door. After two months of the house share with James, our friendship broke down. Someone had

41

entered our room and stolen money from our reserves. James blamed me; he thought I had stolen it. This breach of trust was something I could not reconcile with. I eventually moved into a new house in another neighbourhood with Anna.

*

My mother had sent me to Yaoundé to live with my sister Ndinge for a year in 1992. (My sister was never married, like my mother she too had boyfriends who came and went.) My sister's house was adjacent to a coffin production facility that specialised in coffins for children; they had these coffins on full display, I was terrified. As a result, I spent most of my time at my uncle's house as he lived just a stone's throw away. The house was always full of my uncles and nephews and it was here that I learned to play Scrabble and became a local champion. It was also here that I fell in love with Enjema. I might have to pay a Titkoli (a fine imposed by the chief for wrong doing) when this book is published as Enjema and I are technically related— she is the daughter of my grandfather's brother. Does that count?

It was in Yaoundé that I lost my virginity to a Bayangi (a small tribe in southern Cameroon) prostitute in Obili; giving my virginity to a prostitute cost me one pound.

Chapter 6

By some miracle, we had made it into summer but my relationship with Stars had deteriorated. There was this beautiful girl. She walked gracefully whenever she'd approach us at the petrol station. She was completely out of my league but Stars believed he had a chance and asked me to tell her that he fancied her. I could not bring myself to do it.

One day she invited me to her village. There was a young soldier who used to hang around the garage who agreed to drive us there. After she had visited her parents, we sat by a pond together; with the sound of frogs croaking, it reminded me of back home where the whole village bathed during summer. It was a perfect setting for romance and we shared our first kiss. Unfortunately our young driver explained to Stars what had transpired between the girl and I and I was given the sack. I pleaded with Stars to no avail; I had made an enemy. Fortunately Anna never found out and one day after dinner, she made a marital proposal; she'd bought and engraved two rings with 'My Love Forever' and so I became engaged. She was a brilliant cook and all she expected from me was to pay a share of the rent. I was happy and temporarily forgot about my plight, though that plight would soon return as I was desperate for work.

I was soon contacted by Edwin, who still lived at the hostel, who told me some businessmen had arrived from Moscow and were interested in my services as a translator.

On my way to the hostel a green Audi pulled to a stop and Valodia and his wife Lola, beckoned me. This couple had been extremely generous to me during my time at the petrol station— the minimum tip I received from them was twenty roubles.

'Where are you going?' asked Valodia.

'I am going to the hostel,' I replied.

'We're going for a picnic, come with us?' Before I could ponder, Lola got out of the passenger seat and opened the backdoor. I hesitated at first then thought: 'A picnic, why not?' Instead of sitting in the front with her husband, Lola joined me in the back seat. As the car drove off, Lola started caressing my leg. I looked in the side-mirror and the husband made eye contact and gave me a wry smile. Lola then kissed my neck, ear lobe and then my mouth.

I am a village boy, from the foothills of Mount Cameroon, my clansmen are divided across Buea, more importantly I am from the village of Wovilla in Small Soppo. When I was growing up, I never saw Mola Njoh kissing Aunty Frida or my mother kissing another man in public, in fact open displays of affection were frowned upon. Now here I was in a small corner of Russia, in Stavropol, in a layby indulging in sexual intercourse with Lola whilst her husband watched. I was on the brink of ejaculation when the husband leaned over and kissed me on the lips. I knew this was witchcraft and I was being initiated. We were in the layby for a good few hours, only interrupted by some squirrels and the need for Lola to indulge herself in the consumption of strawberries.

Valodia, with his bits dangling in front of me (I had never seen an uncircumcised penis before) said, 'You know Eric, my wife really likes you. We have another girl, Tania is her name, she's twenty years old, she forms part of our repertoire.'

I didn't go to the hostel that evening, instead they dropped me by Anna's bread shop and I went to visit James. After telling James what had happened, he phoned Edwin and Loretta, who both came to visit us pronto.

Again, I told the story how I had engaged in a three-way sex act with a man and his wife. Edwin and Loretta were in total shock. When I told them the husband had kissed me on the lips, they agreed this was witchcraft. Edwin went to the supermarket and

44

bought some lemon grass and peppermint leaves, they were boiled together and placed in a bowl, and I covered myself with a thick blanket and inhaled the fumes. All this time Edwin, James and Loretta were doing some ancient incantations, inviting the spirits of my ancestors to leave their warm graveyards in Wovilla and come to Stavropol. To them, I needed rescue. Obviously, their attempts at inviting the spirit of my ancestors failed as I went with Valodia and Lola on three further occasions.

When I was introduced to the businessmen from Moscow (two Cameroonians and two Nigerians) I was told my task was to translate what they had to say to local businessmen in Stavropol. For this, I would be paid a percentage of what they made on their deal. This was all that was required of me, so I accepted without question. I was happy; I felt blessed and privileged to be able to speak the Russian language, now opportunities were coming my way.

Our day consisted of visiting luxurious shopping malls, bars and cafés. I could not believe what these guys were saying—such an easy job. Finally my prayers had been answered, I could raise enough money to make my way back to Cameroon.

Our group included a fellow Cameroonian called Alphonse, another guy we had simply given the nickname 'the President', and two Ibo Nigerians, travelling with Cameroonian passports. The Ibo boys had been brought to Cameroon as young children and had spent all their lives working as 'boy boys' (child slaves) for their Oga's (wealthy businessmen). They had amassed enough money to buy a passage to Europe but, like myself, they too had been caught up in the human trafficking scam. In their hopelessness and despair they became small-time cocaine dealers in Moscow. It was a bad time, however, to enter such a trade in Moscow; as we watched television, we saw raid after raid by armed police breaking into houses containing Africans. We saw people jumping into the Moscow rivers in attempts to escape the long arm of the law. I had heard about drugs but at this stage I was naïve and still never indulged.

Despite the risks, Alphonse's two men had managed to make a small amount of money and were the main sponsors of this business trip to Stavropol. However, they did not have selling drugs on their mind, their plan to make money involved a rather ingenious scam.

Their chat-up line revolved around the statement, 'We have a dollar making machine!' Of course there was no such machine but the very mention of a process that churned out dollars got potential clients interested straightaway.

It wasn't anything like the internet scams that Cameroonians and Nigerians are famous for, what these guys were proposing was far more simplistic. All you need is a capital of three, one-hundred-dollar bills in order to convince a client how genuine and how easy it is to get rich with such a scheme. The client is asked to provide three one-hundred-dollar bills. To gain the trust of the client, it is suggested that all the transactions take place at the client's house. It was that simple. The truth is, if these guys had approached me, and I had money, I would have fallen for this scam. I was convinced by how genuine they came across. I fell for it big time. There is a saying that goes, 'If something sounds too good to be true...'

The Scam

The first step is to dress to impress. This means buying expensive clothing, complete with handkerchief poking out of your top pocket to project the aura of wealth. Then you need to speak gently and slowly, choosing your words carefully; the rest is easy. You tell your victim that for an investment of one thousand dollars, you would offer them two thousand dollars in return. The only capital you need for this scam is three hundred dollars (in three, one-hundred-dollar bills), plain paper cut to the size of a dollar bill, some iodine, a syringe, protective gloves, warm water and detergent.

You start by pouring the iodine onto the blank dollar bill-sized paper. The iodine turns the paper blue. You then ask the client for two clean one-hundred-dollar bills, which you also cover in iodine and place either side of the blank. You then place the bills in a small plastic bag and compress between two heavy books and place in a freezer – what the client doesn't know is you have switched the package for one containing three genuine bills.

Once all the exchanges are complete, you return three days later and, using warm water and some detergent, wash up your previously packaged dollar bills removing the iodine. The client is left bemused when three genuine bills appear. To amplify his curiosity, you insist on taking him to the money exchange centre and exchanging the dollars to prove that they are authentic. The person working at the exchange centre will check to see whether the bills are forgeries or not. You know the money is legitimate but the client thinks they are forgeries.

As there are still some iodine stains on the money, the person behind the exchange centre looks repeatedly at the bills. They take longer than usual; the client is getting anxious until eventually the money is exchanged.

Of course, when you carry out the main scam the bundle is much bigger and contains blank bill-sized paper previously soaked in iodine and stained blue—you will be miles away before they are washed in warm water and still blank! It's all about sleight of hand and switching packages. To bewilder the client, you can get small medicine bottles, fill them up with mixed versions of homemade detergent and label them with complex chemical formulas.

Once the client accepts your proposal, everything else becomes administrative. How much are they willing to invest? When can they invest? You must make sure there's a limited time frame between the demonstration and when the actual deal takes place as some clients have the tendency to ask questions of extended family members, who might put doubts into their minds. As I have said, it is too good to be true... At every stage of the demonstration, the client must be reminded of the expensive nature of the chemicals involved.

Our first client was an Armenian gentleman who ran a small liquor store. He was easily hooked and after a small demonstration in his dacha, he invited us to his house where he said he would invest one thousand dollars. The package is supposed to remain intact for three days in a freezer under a heavy weight to encourage bonding but, in his excitement, the Armenian opened the package on the same night. When he telephoned us to explain what had happened, we told him unfortunately, because air had gotten into the package, there was nothing we could do about the situation. He pleaded for his money back but the guys turned the argument around to suggest we had lost our chemicals so he owed us. We never heard from the Armenian again. For my role as the translator I was given two hundred dollars.

As a translator, I had to testify that the business proposal was genuine—there was no one in Stavropol at the time that could threaten my place as a translator—and they believed my every word.

*

I remember my little dog; I had named it Meki Me Ngalle (Meki, the son of Ngalle). I loved Meki with every part of my being. My mother had paid two thousand CFA Francs for me to secure the dog, all I had to do was to wait until Meki was weaned from his mother but I could not wait that long so when Meki was only three weeks old I brought him home. It took him an age to settle as he kept disappearing, going back to his mother for some milk. This carried on for a while until eventually he got used to me. Meki, like Evenya'a Mboli, followed me around; I had a new friend. He followed me to the farm. When I went to wash my uniform in the streams of Mosre, Meki followed me.

When I came home from school Meki would know and he would

48

come at full speed from the back of Mola Ngombi's compound and jump all over me. Meki was brown and had permanent marks under his eyes, as if he had been crying—he had the face of a mother leopard whose children had been taken captive by hunters. Meki was a brilliant hunting dog. I remember one afternoon one of my nephews, Augustin, and I took Meki hunting along the streams of Mosre. We came across a perfect hunting spot; deep holes had been freshly dug and we saw fresh rat mole droppings, half chewed palm nuts and freshly collected dried leaves in little bundles—all tell-tale signs we were in rat mole country.

We collected some heavy stones and placed them on top of some of the holes, and then focussed our attention on just one hole. It had an exit and entry that was just elbow length deep. Meki started barking loudly, he paused to place his head deep into this hole and barked even louder. Augustine folded his sleeves to his elbow, bent down and reached deep into the hole.

'Eric,' he said with joy on his face, 'I can feel something. It's soft.' Normally, in this situation, we would use dried palm leaves, some firewood and matove (palm nut chafes) to start a fire and smoke the rat mole out. I jumped around with excitement; we had Meki and knew there was no hiding place for the rat mole. Regardless of what our mothers cooked, catching an animal in the forest was automatic pepper soup. Augustine placed his hands inside again and poked the animal. My heart was pumping faster and faster, I rolled up my sleeve, bent down on my knees and reached inside the hole, I could feel what Augustine had felt. I poked it, it felt soft. The one thing that saved us was the fact that the animal had turned its head and was facing the direction of Meki, who barked louder—we were touching and playing with one of the most dangerous animals in Cameroon, if not in the whole of the African continent. Even when we heard the hissing noise, we didn't know what it was, we only got excited, confirming our suspicions that there was an animal in the hole; we poked and poked and the hissing only got Meki even more excited and he barked louder. Suddenly Meki reached deep into the hole and pulled out what I now know was a Bitis Nasicornis or Rhinoceros Viper. That was when it dawned on us, we had been dicing with death; it was only when I was in our housing estate flat in Ely and watching David Attenborough that I learned the noise a snake like that would make when issuing a warning.

As soon as the snake came out, it bit Meki on the side of the head. The snake didn't even bother running, it just curled itself up and retracted into a bundle, still hissing. It was fat, having gone into the hole and eaten mother rat mole and her little ones and claimed the hole as its new abode for the foreseeable future, while it digested its meal. We had come and disturbed its tranquillity and Meki had suffered the consequences.

Meki stopped barking and began making faint whimpering noises—he was crying while looking dazed. He staggered, losing his balance, as his hind legs had gone wobbly, like a car that had lost its passenger side wheel. Augustine and I were stunned, frightened to the core. The snake adjusted its head, which had two horns, and stared at us in a relaxed and suspicious way. I could see it rolling its eyes; it flicked its tongue and opened its mouth, as if it was saying something, probably telling us to back off. I couldn't run, walk or even scream. Augustine looked so shocked you would have thought the snake had bitten him. After what seemed a good few minutes, we shouted in unison, 'Meki!'

He was nowhere to be seen. We shouted and shouted and our shouting reached the humble abode of Mola Maimbe, a village hunter and a part time juju man. He knew something was amiss, as he brought his spear and a machete. The rhinoceros viper just lay there, looking at us, daring us to make a move. Mola Maimbe speared the viper. The spear went through its skin and into the ground, pinning the viper on one spot; it spun around but it was stuck. Then using the back of his machete, he whacked the viper on its head until he was satisfied it was dead. Maimbe then gathered a few palm leaves and using village craftsmanship, produced a small basket, and loaded the snake into it and carried it on his shoulder. He later told us, when

50

preparing it for pepper soup, what he found in the snake's stomach—the viper had beaten us to the rat mole.

We had escaped from the jaws of death and I mean this literally as everyone who had been bitten by a snake in the village had died. When I got home, I found Meki under my bed. He was dying. I called his name but he could only muster enough energy to shake his tail. We do not have enough hospitals to cater for humans, let alone dogs. My dog was dying in front of me. I sat down on the huge stone outside my mother's kitchen, which had been deposited there by the volcanic eruption of Mount Cameroon in 1922, and cried. I was scared of touching Meki, in case I got poisoned, so I could not soothe his pain. If only I was a juju man. The only option I had was to contact Pa Takesh. I had not spoken to him since he had killed my goat and I hated him but now he was the only one who could save Meki.

As I was about to make my way to Pa Takesh's house, I saw another villager called Tapotto, (I later heard he died of a lung disease because of afforforh, the Cameroonian equivalent of homemade vodka, abuse, or maybe it was witchcraft.) Tapotto was an expert in traditional medicine and I had grown to love and respect Tapotto, he was close friends with my sister Ndinge and had helped lay down the foundations of her house in my mother's compound. I told Tapotto what had happened and gave him a detailed description of the snake. Tapotto paused when I said it had a soft underbelly and he asked, 'How you know it had a soft belly?' I told him whilst it was still in the hole, Augustine and I had been poking it. He screamed, 'Oh my God, child, have you lost your senses? Have you lost your head? Were you trying to kill yourself?'

Shaking his head, puzzled, looking at me he walked past the kitchen and disappeared to the back of the compound, towards the gate where Pa Takesh had killed Evenya'a Mboli. After what seemed like an age, Tapotto came back with two peelings of bark from a tree in his hands. He checked Meki's head, which was getting bigger and bigger, his eyes full of mucous. Meki was crying and in excruciating pain and I was crying with him. Tapotto reassured me that if the poison had not reached Meki's heart, he could save him. He loosely tied the two peelings round Meki's neck and promised to come back in a couple of days to check on him. I had resigned myself to the fact that it was only a matter of time before Meki kicked the bucket.

That evening, Tapotto came to the house and told my mother I had been putting my hands inside a hole that housed a rhinoceros viper. I was sat on the ewongo and my mother leapt up and gave me a slap. She said, 'If you want to kill yourself, wait until I am gone, you child of ill omen.'

I could not sleep as Meki's grunts kept me awake. The whole compound was sad, as everyone loved Meki. The next day Meki's head swelled more. I did not go to college, I counted the days until Tapotto came back and I prayed for Meki not to die. To convince my mother I was going to school, I put on my uniform in the morning and walked up to my father's, waited an hour and returned home as by then my mother would have left for work. On the third day, Tapotto came to visit Meki as promised.

The dog could not move—his head was humongous whilst the rest of his body shrivelled like an Ethiopian mushroom. Meki was dying. We dragged Meki gently from under the bed and brought him onto the veranda. Tapotto came prepared and using sharp razors, he cut open Meki's jaws and neck. Thick green liquid poured out with each cut. Tapotto collected the concoction dripping out of Meki's skin onto a coco leaf that he had shaped into a cup. Tapotto told me just a drop of that concoction in the water supply could kill the whole village. Meki lay still, helpless and weak. The contents collected in the leaf were carried by Tapotto and poured into our latrine. Meki looked like a monster in a horror movie; he looked horrid.

Using traditional techniques, Tapotto managed to save my dog's life—I was forever in his debt. Within a few days, Meki had made a total recovery. We played together, we went hunting together but he never placed his head into another hole.

*

Our second client pulled out of the business, we had insisted the smallest amount was five thousand dollars, they could not afford it, or maybe they'd smelt foul play.

Chapter 7

At this time I was torn between the two women in my life—I liked Anna but I loved Lola, the beautiful one. Anna wanted me to stay in Russia with her and start a family whilst Lola was fascinated with the notion of visiting the continent of Africa with me. Her favourite animal was the wildebeest and she asked if I had come across any. She pictured Africa as this large land where animals roamed everywhere.

*

I saw crocodiles every Sunday in the Ndian River as we crossed the Bulu bridge to attend mass at the Catholic church. Crossing that bridge was treacherous, it was dreadful, planks had fallen off it in places and dangled down. If we had had health and safety inspectors, they would have closed that bridge in an instant. We dreaded Sundays.

My mother sent me to live with my sister because she believed that her accident was brought on by the villagers who wanted to kill her and, since they couldn't get her, they would turn their attention on me. In Mundemba, we kept an alligator just behind the kitchen. It was huge and we had its mouth tied permanently but one afternoon the alligator stretched its mouth muscles and all the ropes came off. This frightened my nephew so much that he said his first words. That afternoon, my sister's husband killed the alligator and we had pepper soup that day (pepper soup is a delicacy, usually eaten when the weather is cold, that is simple to cook and relies upon pepper, salt, onions, Maggi cubes for seasoning, and whatever meat you choose to add).

One of my rites of passage as a boy was to learn how to set traps, my favourite being what we called fence traps. It is very simple: using sticks leaves and twigs, you construct an average height fence, however you leave little gaps in the fence for animals to squeeze through. The problem is these gaps have snares or traps—any slight movement will trigger the snare and the animal will be caught. On my way I passed an old man called Lorkhorlorkor. It was an ill omen for Lorkhorlorkor was known in the village as a witchcraft practitioner and was feared by all, young and old alike; he was the last person you would want to come across. In fact, when he died, it is rumoured that he had his head separated and buried far away from his body; this only added to his mysticism. Our village felt like a ghost town after six o'clock for there were rumours that Lorkhorlorkor's decapitated body had been seen sitting outside his house.

I had been checking my trap and for some time but nothing had happened; I thought this afternoon was not going to be any different but seeing Lorkhorlorkor and the way he'd looked at me (even when Lorkhorlorkor was not looking in your direction, you still felt his gaze) increased my apprehension.

The first and second traps were as I had seen them previously, however, the third trap looked like it had been disturbed. I noticed the grass had been flattened then I saw the tail end of a snake that I recognised straight away as a green mamba. We grew up surrounded by tales of people being bitten by snakes who never made it to the hospital, so we were wary of snakes and extremely frightened of mambas. Mola Maimbe, a local hunter, had told us that mambas commuted in pairs, male and female.

There was a tree that had fallen and become hollow with age, and every afternoon two black mambas would come out and enjoy the sun. I had seen them quite a few times and was no longer frightened of them. In fact, I was certain by now the two snakes recognised me; we made eye contact every time I walked past that tree and I was more frightened if I didn't see the snakes. We had developed some sort of mutual admiration and respect, they knew I meant them no harm *and they reciprocated. I was just a farm boy and the two mambas had become my guardians. Mola Maimbe had also told us that if you noticed a mamba in your trap, you should walk slowly backwards, get some stones and sticks and make some loud noise to scare the mate who might be lurking nearby. So I slowly retreated, got a few stones and a long stick and followed the routine as I was told.*

I then gathered some courage and approached the snake. In order to ensure it was dead, we had been told to hit on the head with force. I lifted the stick and brought it down towards the snake's head with all the force I could muster. However, in the process of lifting and bringing down the stick, an mbetetu (beetle) sprayed its pepper spray into my eyes. It hurt like hellfire. Maybe Lorkhorlorkor had placed a curse on me for I completely missed the snake's head, cutting the snare and unleashing one pissed-off green mamba. If you think Usain Bolt is fast, you should have seen me that day. My legs never touched the ground, and somehow, I managed to invoke a flying juju (spell) that ensured I flew all the way to my grandfather's compound without touching the ground.

*

If it is true what they say about one in two hundred men being direct descendants of Genghis Khan, then Batu and his friend Arban had that genetic link. Their stature was imposing; they both had clean-shaven heads like monks and they both looked a bit Mongolian with extremely strong palms and handshakes. It all made sense when Arban told us that as a teenager he had spent time in Siberia digging snow and making illegal homemade vodka known as 'Samagon'.

During winter, he told us, the price goes up and he and his brother capitalised on it. This was how they had made their fortunes before moving to Stavropol where they ran a successful liquor store. They also had a small summer business importing watermelons from Uzbekistan. (Anthony was doing the same importing of watermelons into Sochi from Dagestan, however, his watermelons were drained and filled with a certain white powder.)

Batu, Arban and some unknown companions came to the hostel around 8 p.m. in a convoy of cars. Their companions never spoke a single word; they wore black trousers and black leather jackets and carried man-bags. Alphonse, the President and I drove with Arban and Batu for a couple of hours; we left civilisation behind us completely. By the time we got to our destination it was total darkness. Arban and Batu were excited at the prospect of doubling their money after just three days, and they had brought with them an initial capital of five thousand dollars with a promissory note that if the business were successful, they would bring fifty thousand dollars for a one-off transaction.

I was getting really scared—the only comparable fear had been seeing that green mamba and now here I was in the middle of nowhere, with people who looked like killers. They had strong astute faces, which when they spoke, remained straight—there was no betrayal of emotions.

I was far away from my village, far away from the meandering slopes of Small Soppo. No longer surrounded by the plantains behind my mother's house. I could no longer go and steal pears from Mola Ngombis farm; I could not just go and hide in the strawberry fields behind the kitchen; I could not just disappear for hours eating sugarcane and pineapple at Mola Mongambe's farm. My village only existed in dreams, I was playing the role of an innocent translator trying to scam five thousand dollars from people who could kill us and abandon our corpses in the middle of a forest and no one would have been any the wiser.

We had left the main road, crossed little streams and climbed a few hills before arriving in the middle of a large compound. The sky was in perfect darkness. We came across a small hut with a single light bulb above the door with lots of moths banging their heads on it in some sort of dazed craze. Arban indicated to me that it was the toilet.

From outside, the house was baronial. Though built from wood, it was humongous and elevated from the ground by huge pillars. Two German Shepherd dogs greeted us on chains barking as if they had sensed our intention. Above the entrance was an imposing skull of a stag; Arban later told us he was a seasoned hunter and proudly showed us his plethora of guns and ammunition, which included an elephant rifle. I had seen one of those when I attended a funeral of my mother's uncle. My mother had explained to me that it was customary to fire a gun to shoo the bad spirits away.

I whispered to Alphonse, 'Do you think it's a clever idea us attempting to take money from these people?'

But Alphonse and The President were adamant saying, 'We're here now, we must finish what we started.'

Inside, the house was well appointed with fine silk curtains and beautiful rugs. Arban gave us a tour of the house: skulls of various animal covered the walls, there was a huge piano and above the television was an imposing picture of Mikhail Gorbachev, which Arban pointed to and said, 'One of our own.'

The men in black jackets waited outside.

I was scared but not terribly afraid. I was already dead, my fathers' relatives in Cameroon had killed me, I was decapitated, I was a headless chicken and my fate had been decided. I had no control over my life: whatever direction the wind blew, that was where I went. We settled in the dining room—they had killed and roasted a whole lamb and there was baked bread directly from the oven as well as salted fish, beer and vodka but like all good businessmen, we postponed the merriment until we had finished the business at hand.

One of the guys in black jackets was summoned into the house and given some instructions; he disappeared and came back after a few minutes with a bag that was handed to Arban. I looked across at Batu and it looked like he had developed some doubts. Arban opened the bag and brought out a brown envelope that contained five thousand dollars. Alphonse counted the money just to confirm and reassure them that we knew what we were doing. My heart was beating fast; I had never seen that amount of money before. As Alphonse counted, Batu reached into the bag and placed a hand gun onto the table. Without betraying or moving any muscle on his face he said, 'If you lie to us, we will kill you.' I translated the dire warning to Alphonse and The President but they just laughed and dismissed it saying, 'Never.'

I was translating very well but my mouth and throat were getting dry.

As if drawn by the intense silence and strain on our faces, a moth fluttered towards us. I suddenly wished I had wings like that moth so I could fly away. A small drama began to unfold between Batu and the moth—every time the moth flew towards him, he waved the back of his hand in an attempt to kill it but the winged intruder avoided the danger until it landed on the ceiling, sealing its fate. Its fluttering about was being monitored by a wall gecko, as soon as it landed the gecko swallowed the moth whole with a fast launch of its tongue. Batu smiled and Arban laughed out loud while The President concentrated on building the bundle of cash, mixing their five thousand dollars with our fake dollars.

*

I remember the afternoon so very well, it was a Saturday and Morake, the second son of my adopted Sister Monjowa and I had gone fishing in the small springs of Mosre. All the villagers have at one time or another fished in Mosre water and no matter how hot the weather was, the water remained cold.

Morake and I had been fishing for tadpoles and crabs—the waters were so serene and cold that afternoon, it seemed as though it had impacted on the metabolisms of the creatures. It was like we'd hit the jackpot as every stone we lifted had a small crab underneath for which that day was marked; they were destined for the charcoal. The tadpoles were easy to catch and most times we just used our hands.

We caught bucket loads that day. There were no happier times in my life than spending them in the open with Morake. I love Morake, we are connected spiritually. Despite the things that unfolded, that cord which attaches Morake and I has never been severed. In fact, when I came to Wales Morake wrote me a personal letter, the content of which made me cry and still does.

We were excited as we walked past my mother's house up the road to my father's compound. As luck would have it, it had rained slightly that afternoon and rainwater had collected itself in some old moulded bricks on the side of the house. This was our temporary fishpond. The rest of the tadpoles and crabs we wrapped in banana leaves after marinating with a dash of salt and pepper.

Aunty Ewuwe was in the kitchen cooking Mbasri in Mbanga soup and she took the wrapped tadpoles and crabs and placed them into the hot charcoal while we went outside and played hopscotch. A few minutes later Aunty Ewuwe shouted, 'Elickie!' She loved calling me Elickie instead of Eric. Her shouts simply meant our feast was cooked and ready to be served. Morake and I sat at the front of the house and ate our well-prepared catch of the day, every crunch of crab was met by the extra sweet and soft tadpole melting; it was a little piece of heaven. We licked our fingers ignoring the attentions of the jealous weaverbird that had nested just outside Mr Enongene's house. Yet the weaverbird was wiser than us: it had identified our improvised fishpond. We wondered why it kept flying back and forth, and we found out too late the bastard had smuggled most of the tadpoles and used them to fatten his family.

While Morake and I rested on a mat on the veranda, Mola Isaac (a paternal uncle) walked past us brusquely without his normal charming smile, in fact I do not think he even noticed us. His behaviour was quite strange as I was his favourite boy. The sun was out and hot. I had helped prune Mola Isaac's tomato plants; he had such a beautiful tomato garden. I loved to climb his mango and guava tree. His children were sisters to me, in fact when Mola Isaac's wife abandoned him with all his children, we supported him.

Mola Isaac went straight into the kitchen and spoke with Aunty Ewuwe. Whatever was said between Mola Isaac and Aunty Ewuwe saw me tumbling from the top of a hill, nonstop, dropping fast like a terrified tortoise dropped at extreme height by an eagle.

Then my aunt called out, 'Morake! Hurry up and come here!' I didn't think anything of it, I just thought Morake was in trouble, and whatever it was must have been quite serious. I waited for maybe ten or fifteen minutes but Morake never came out and there was no crying. I knew for a fact that no one had died for there would have been tears and wailings from far away. I went to go inside but the front and the back door of the house were locked. When I knocked Aunty Ewuwe opened the door slowly, her eyes were red—as if she had spent all afternoon blowing fire with her mouth and all the smoke had taken up residence inside – and she said these words, words in Bakweri, words that have haunted me ever since; I hear her voice most nights. It was a harbinger of danger, a bearer of terrible news.

She said, 'Ngalle you are no longer welcomed in this compound. You are not allowed to play with Morake. You are no longer a member of this family. If you ever set foot in this compound again, you will see what I will do to you.'

I tried to force my way into the kitchen to see what Morake was doing, he had his head on his knees and seemed to be crying. Mola Isaac's eyes were like a bloody cloth, he looked at me as a lion would a wounded prey, I saw danger in his eyes, I saw a semblance of death. He looked so angry, his anger seemed to have polished his face of every wrinkle, and his face was darker than a treacherous moon. I was shocked; what was it that I had done to deserve such bestial hostility? I didn't know what to make of this; I could not fathom what had just taken place—my aunt and uncle were too old to be playing an April Fool's joke.

That was the last time Morake and I shared a smile, it was also the last time I saw him. I was suddenly a plague, I was an outcast, every time I walked past my father's house, if there was someone at the front or simply resting on the Veranda, they would look at me with such disdain and go inside shutting the door behind them.

I tried walking towards my mother's house but my knees were unable to carry my bodyweight. As I walked over the small bridge it seemed to be experiencing a tremor, I was panicking so much. Moki Monyama would later tell me that I walked like someone who was in a trance or who had seen a ghost, normally I would stop and chat, but on this day, I just walked towards my mother's kitchen.

Mola Pa Takesh and Late Etongo were talking about the latest antics of the Obassinjom which was an imported juju brought from the Bakossi land by the village elders to help protect the village against Mami and Papa Waters—those ungodly spirits that only came out at night to wreak havoc on the whole village. The Obassinjom was not doing a very good job, for whatever had come over my Aunty Ewuwe and Mola Isaac was more than witchcraft, it was madness.

As I approached our kitchen, I saw my mother sitting with her back towards the door, this again was extremely strange as my mother always sits next to the fireside but today, she was sitting with her back against the entrance and my younger sister, Queenta, was in her chair. When I walked in, I went and sat by the Ewongo (an indoor kraal were the goats slept at night). My mother had a letter in her hand, she had her snuff stained handkerchief in her right hand and she was crying. My little sister, Queenta, also had tears on her cheeks.

*

Our silence was punctuated by a question now and then from Arban such as, 'How long have you guys been doing this?' He had a childlike joy on his face, he knew in his heart they had found a jackpot, two black men who they'd just met, introducing them to an easy money-making system. He loved me for making the introduction. I was the naïve translator who, for a small percentage, was going to make both parties wealthy. After around two hours The President finished building the package.

We had asked Arban to buy some syringes, gloves—one of the tricks is to inform the client that the chemicals are highly corrosive—and an industrial type tape. The President then reached into his shoulder bag and retrieved a small bottle that had been sealed but soft enough in the middle for a syringe to burst through. He then delivered the first dosage and it was now left for Alphonse to put on his gloves and carry the package and place it into the freezer, which had already been emptied by Arban as we had asked.

Alphonse carried the package with extreme care and placed it in the freezer. The guys standing outside were then called inside and we sat down and enjoyed the food and drank the vodka. Conversation flowed. Whilst we ate, the package was brought from the freezer to the table for two more doses. Between the second and third dosage, The President had switched their package with our own that we had prepared at the hostel. Then The President asked for everyone to be quiet as he wanted to say a toast, looking directly into my eyes, he said, 'Grumbeaf dey inside box trap.'

I stuttered at first, realising what The President meant. I turned around to Arban, Batu and their two friends and said, 'Let us drink to our ancestors.'

This was all I could come up with, however The President had just told me in street pidgin that he had switched the package and he had the money. Arban and his entourage lifted their vodka glasses and toasted, 'To our ancestors.'

We drank and ate knowing that we had their money and they had our iodine soaked fake dollar bills that were worth less than a rotten apple. We were given a lift back to the hostel while the other guys, including Batu, had stayed behind, guarding what they thought was their quick way of becoming millionaires. Arban promised to pick us up on Saturday evening so we could stay at their dacha and open the package together first thing Sunday morning. Arban was so excited, saying the next transaction should be for fifty thousand dollars, as he was going to bring some of his business friends in on the deal.

When I got back to the house, in the early hours in the morning, Anna was half asleep and I snuggled into bed. That morning she was excited to see me and we made love repeatedly. The money was split equally. For a few hours of translation I had earned one thousand dollars. 'Geez, can life be this easy?' I asked myself. I gave my friend Saul one hundred dollars. He wanted to follow us to Moscow. I pleaded with him not to because of the images of Cameroonians being chased with dogs and swimming in the Rivers of Moscow flashed in my mind. That was the last time I spoke with Saul.

It was time for me to get out. I had a perfect plan. I was going to go to Moscow, head to the Cameroonian Embassy and ask to be repatriated back home to Cameroon. I so much wanted to confront my father's ghost, I wanted to stand upon my father's grave and shout out loud, I wanted to wake him up from his deep slumber, I wanted to question sister Monjowa, I wanted to challenge Mola Isaac. Most especially, I wanted to talk with my aunty, my father's sister, I wanted to ask her about such unbridled betrayal.

*

My aunty and I use to go up to the lower regions of Mount Fako, to dig for Cocoyams, then, whilst the rest of the children played, I would help her cook in the kitchen. We cooked all kinds of food. I grew up thinking of my aunty as my second mother. I loved visiting her in Wonya Morake, especially during school holidays. In Wonya Morake, I was the 'boy boy' or 'slave'. It never bothered me as I knew my challenging work would be rewarded.

I was told to fetch water—I always prayed for rainfall to spare me the weight of carrying a pot full of water, which weighed as much as a bag of cement, about ten times a day. I did the dishes and I washed all the clothes. I became an expert carpet cleaner. It was also here that I first counted to eleven in French and it was among my father's side of the family that I watched my first perfect film, The Sound of Music. *Before I returned to my mother's village, I would be given one thousand CFA francs, sometimes five thousand, the equivalent of seven pounds. When my aunty could not afford to give me money, she ensured I had one of my nephew's T-shirts, and she made me her favourite dish, ekwang (this food is mysterious and takes the ingenuity of a goddess to perfect it). My father's family loved me; of this I had no doubt.*

*

There were no direct trains to Moscow from Stavropol so we booked the next best thing, a train from Stavropol to Krasnodar and then from Krasnodar to Moscow. I convinced the guys that because of the long route the tickets were fifty dollars each but they were only twenty-five dollars each; nothing had changed.

We said our goodbyes and left the hostel just before 11 a.m. because we could not risk Arban and his friend turning up early. We left one at a time and met on the other side of the university instead of going towards the bus stop, our usual route. We figured if Arban and his entourage were waiting for us, they would have been waiting just outside the main entrance.

The journey was smooth, until we were stopped by five police officers that insisted on searching us. When they discovered that we all had money belts, they got excited as they thought we were smuggling drugs and took us to their station to interview us. Again my Russian came into play as I told them we were attending a seminar on human rights organised by the university and that I was the student union president. I spoke their language flawlessly and they believed me, even telling me to pass on to my travelling companions the need to speak the language. They then drove us to the train station where we boarded our train to Moscow. As the train left the station, I remembered saying au revoir to my mother at the airport in Douala.

*

She did not look into my eyes and, when I looked at her, I realised she was crying; she did not want me to notice her tears. I had been separated from my mother a couple of times before but there was something strange about this separation—I was elated. I was leaving the cesspit of crime that had become my patriarchal inheritance, yet I was given hope, an olive branch, I was going to the land paved with gold, the land built on the backbone and sweat of my ancestors buried in shallow graves; I was going to the land where the spirits of my ancestors linger.

I was happy I was leaving my paternal ancestral shrine behind but seeing one's mother cry is never a good sight and for a moment I thought maybe staying at home, resigning myself to fate, was the best option. But I had all these demons inside of me struggling to come out and it would have been madness if I had stayed.

My mother hugged me, still avoiding my gaze, then she took my hands into hers and slowly and steadily, she gave each of my fingers a gentle bite, paying tribute to a village adage, sealing the fact that the thoughts of my relatives and ancestors would be with me and that the spirit of our dearest departed would guide me—that God would answer the tears and laments of Abel.

I almost burst into tears but I was embarking upon an important journey and a combination of joy and sorrow within me revealed itself through a faint smile. I can still see my sister's husband Mr Ndanga, my small group of friends who looked utterly amazed that I was leaving Cameroon—they thought I was a man of strength and fortitude but did not know that whatever courage I showed was a front. Internally I was dying with apprehension, nostalgia and most of all the fear that I would never see my mother again. My internal well was filled with tears. Yes, I cried but the tears stayed inside.

Chapter 8

A True Confession

Dear Mr Charles,

I am writing you this letter with regards to the six-bedroom property your father left in his last will and testament. You have been summoned to attend my chambers as your father's will is being challenged by his family and they refute that you are the son of the late Oscar Ngalle Charles. Please attend my chambers with all the necessary documents and witnesses in pursuit of this matter.

Yours Sincerely,

Chief Justice Paul

I have not told anyone about this. Nothing that happened to me during my stay in Russia came close to the devastation I felt on this day inside the courthouse in Buea, in the south-west province of the Republic of Cameroon. On this day, my father died for a second time, and this was the day I died. In Russia I was just a ghost—I was only resurrected in Wales, and even then, it has taken the best part of seventeen years to put this memoir together.

It has taking me seventeen years to sit down and write this chapter for I have written and destroyed it many times in my head; I have played the events that unfolded repeatedly. Even now, as I sit down in Cardiff Central Library to write, I am developing extra wrinkles. I look around and there are fairies inside the library, not a single human being, all fairies. Every time I visit this episode of my life, the one that I had locked up and thrown away the key, I dread the day I was conceived. What mysterious music were the spirits playing on that day? I can see butterflies with human heads beckoning me to come over to other side, calling my name out loud, asking me to come home. One of the butterflies has a bouquet of flowers around its head, which looks like my departed sister. I am suffering from a mental breakdown, I can see myself falling, drifting into the darkest bits of my temporary sojourn here on earth. A beautiful girl smiles at me from the other side of the computer, was it me she was smiling at or am I dreaming? She's smiling, yet I can't even bring myself to smile, and instead I grimace.

*

Home. I was in my mother's kitchen once more and I was sat on the ewongo'o, whilst my mother sat with her back against the kitchen entrance, my younger sister Queenta had dried tears on her cheeks, the eerie silence was invasive. My mother handed me a letter addressed to Mr Eric Ngalle Charles, the letter was from Chief Justice Paul of the Courts of Justice and Peace, Buea, South West Province, Republic of Cameroon. It was as if all the lizards of the village knew of my impending demise, for they too had congregated and were holding their own conference on the beam that ran around the kitchen. It was as if the weaverbirds, which had built a colony on the jackfruit tree behind my mother's kitchen, had dreamt of this day, for they too were silent.

I spent the best part of my childhood with my late paternal grandmother, Mbamba Mary Mezruwe, in this house. I ate food from the fireside that formed our family shrine in this house. I slept in the room where my father died in this house. I must admit it was a terrifying experience sleeping in that room. I was so scared my mind would form images of different people who had passed on to join our ancestors, these images would then turn into skeletons. I saw shadows moving around the room—we had no lights just a small kerosene lamp that I had to switch off before sleeping. I would not sleep and feigned tears until my grandmother came to sing me a lullaby—she ended up sleeping in the room with me. I tended to my father's grave just behind the kitchen. I loved his family and they loved me. Then the letter from Chief Justice Paul came.

I had been summoned by Chief Justice Paul, the judge had been appointed to determine if I truly was the son of the late Oscar Ngalle Charles, the man I had grown to know and believe to be my father; the man who died eleven months after I was born; the man whose circumstances of death have not made any sense to this day; the man whom the villagers said I was the carbon copy of although I have never seen a picture of my father, nor have I ever encountered his ghost.

My father's death was associated with witchcraft as, apparently, a viper was seen coming out of the kitchen shrine (a specific area in the kitchen reserved for rituals) just underneath the Mbanda (where we smoked meat and keep wood for cooking). Little did my uncle know the snake was my father who was the main guardian of our ancestral shrine.

The snake was killed and a couple of days later, my father started coughing up blood before passing away. My father must have died of a cancerous lung. My mother and I were at his bedside and apparently, just before he died, he whispered something in my ear—I was resting my head on the left side of his chest when he died.

My mother did not have enough money to fight the case properly but she had plenty of support at first from Akwo, who was my father's colleague, who volunteered himself as a witness. Amongst my other witnesses were Mola Etonge, Chief Efange and one or two people who simply started calling me OC as my father's name was Oscar—unfortunately Mola Etonge, who was the village blacksmith, died during the last days of the hearing and never testified.

A lawyer from Elad's Chambers in Buea Town came to represent my mother and we paid what we could afford. Eventually the lawyer started dating my sister and thus represented us as often as he could. I was happy for the services provided by the Elad's chambers, given that their offices were located a stone's throw from my paternal clansmen and women. I was lost in two worlds: that of my father's family and that of my mother.

My mother had a few court luxuries as her sister, my Aunty Ndinge was a court official. Day in, day out, we gathered at Mr Paul's chambers. My mother gave evidence, talking about the circumstances under which she had met my father.

During the hearing, when people were giving evidence, I would cling onto my mother—my body was in pain and I was terrified of the angry looks from my father's side of the family. I was just a boy enjoying my youth. Every day I had to face my father's sister and her powerful entourage—aunts and uncles from both sides and my father's friends. The villagers also attended the hearing, known and unknown faces—they were all there. The case had divided the village right down the middle, it had become the focus of local gossip, saying how dare my mother take on the might of the WonyaMorake, the wealthy segment of what was my father's family. I was terrified, yet these were people I had grown to love unconditionally.

I can still feel Aunty Ndinge patting my back the night before I was at a children's graveyard in New Layout in a town call Tiko. In the middle of the night, in total darkness, under the blackest skies you could imagine, my only companion was one Mr Mbua the juju man. Together we dug open a grave, he had a bottle of beer ready, he would sip and pour some into the grave, an incantation, calling my father's name, before going into a trance, this made the maggots and ants excited. The truth is I never saw my father, not his ghost, not Hamlet's skeleton. I saw a tree move but I am now certain it was my mind playing tricks. I was still terrified.

After gathering a few maggots, some ants and bones, Mola Mbua the juju man mixed them with herbs, which he had prepared earlier, and each joint of my body was slashed open with a razor blade, my blood then dripped onto a machete, not any machete, the one used by palm wine tappers, with a massive head. I am not an Ogbanje child (a child who plagues his or her family with misfortunes. Once recognised as an Ogbanje child you are marked by your family when you die—some children have their nose, ear or even fingers cut off so if you chose to return to the land of the living, you would be recognised.) Instead the juju man was doing this to protect me from what my mother had anticipated as an impending danger. I carry these scars with me as testimony to these events, they are marked all over my body.

As the blood dripped, the juju man rubbed his concoction into my body; it was excruciating. Blood flowed from my wounds onto the machete and slowly into the grave. The ants and maggots increased their pace, sipping on my blood in a mad rush of excitement. At no time during this ritual did I see my father's ghost, a dim light in the distance, and a whiff of cannabis in the air, that was all. I bled.I wished I were stillborn.

Two elephants were fighting, the Kanges, (my mother's family) and the Morakes (my father's family) and I was caught in the middle. It was the price I paid, the price my mother paid for my father's indiscretion, the price my mother was paying for loving one Oscar Ngalle Charles, a father, my father, whose memory was slowly eroding.

I was born out of wedlock you see; does this make me a bastard? The brothers, the sisters, those with whom I ate and danced with, seemed to have had their tongues cut off, they looked at me with such disdain. Suddenly I was a curse, I was to be blamed for all the misfortunes that had befallen the Oscar Ngalle Charles clan. My mother was the most hated woman in the village, for how dare she challenge my father's family? Every evening, village gossipers would congregate and sit at my father's veranda and point mocking fingers at my mother and me as we walked home from the court case. There was no 'hello' nor 'goodbye' from people whom only a week earlier

71

confessed their unconditional love for me and were quite contented that I was growing up to be exactly like my father.

Yes, on the last day of the hearing, my life was flipped upside down, I became a nocturnal being. My eyes were red as the devil himself for truly devils and their henchmen, maybe one or two angels surrounded me. Mr Paul looked at me with the eyes of someone tired, he looked drained, for his eyes had lost their spark. When I first met Chief Justice Paul, I wanted to become a judge. During the week of hearing evidence and counter evidence, like me, Mr Paul had become lifeless, there seemed a complete disconnection between his body and his thoughts. As for me, I was asking questions of myself, I was floating.

On the last day of the hearing Mr Paul, whose voice still rings in my ear, asked my father's family, one at a time, the same question.

'Do you know Eric, the boy sitting next to you?'

Sister Monjowa answered, 'No I don't. I have never seen him before.'

'Do you know Eric, the boy sitting next to you?'

Aunty Ewuwe looked at me intently and said, 'No your honour, I have never seen him before. I do not know him.'

'Do you know Eric, the boy sitting next to you?'

My father's sister looked at me with a face that seemed to suggest I was a wicked child. 'No your honour,' she said, 'I do not know him. I have not seen him before.'

The question was repeated to all the five individuals who were challenging my father's will. As each one said, 'No, I do not know him', I could see Justice Paul shrinking. Every one in my father's family rejected me, they refused any knowledge of me. The judge asked them repeatedly; even he could not fathom the evil that was unfolding. One by one they repeated their answers, 'No, I do not know him.'

With nothing else to do, the judge apologised and asked my mother and I to vacate his chambers and he awarded the property to my father's people. Outside the courthouse my father's family had arranged a traditional dance group to help them celebrate their victor— they even sang and danced to one of my favourite traditional songs.

This was the day I died. It was as if the devil had placed his hands deep in my throat and into my stomach. I had been disembowelled and my entrails dropped to the ground and stampeded upon. I prayed for death and pitied my mother – it would have been better if I had died that day, as the axe forgets what the tree remembers. I have not been able to put the shattered pieces of my heart back together since that day.

Walking home was made more tedious by the fact that the local town crier, a village slag, had carried the news to the village, spreading it like wildfire, and women stood by their doors to greet us and mocked my mother. One old Mamba, who used to call me Oscar Charlie, my father's name, was pointing at my mother as if she wanted to kill her. Yes, that was the day I died, that was the day my soul died, that was the day Satan flew away with me. I became the devil himself. How dare they? Who dares to make my mother cry? My sisters, my aunts, my uncles—they were marked. I was going to initiate a plan. Today I draw in my tears, whilst here in exile in Wales, strangers build thrones in my father's house. I laugh.

Chapter 9

As I looked around and savoured my environment, I no longer felt intimidated by Moscow. I was well dressed and I was starting to feel like a baron; I felt as though I could fly.

I had picked up the Russian tradition of drinking homemade beer with dried and salted fish, so imagine my happiness when I saw a babushka selling such fare. Christmas had come early for the babushka. At first the guys were a bit squeamish but after a few bites and a few sips they were all saying how delicious it was. We stayed on the platform drinking. We drank her keg dry and ate all her fish. She tried offering us semechki, some sort of dried salted pumpkin seeds, it is good but demanding work – it helps when one is bored; so we kindly declined.

Other Russians joined us, some offered us vodka and stayed chatting to us, and the police officers patrolling the station did not bother us, not once. Moscow greeted me with a smile upon my return—this time I was prepared for her, I had money and I had people I knew very well. Out of the corner of my eye I saw two lovers kissing, entangled in a perpetual embrace. I laughed.

'Guys! Guys! Come here.' It was The President calling us. He had used the telephone at the train station to call the hostel in Stavropol. He handed me the telephone and I could hear the voice of one of the students who resided in the hostel on the other end saying that the Russian guys had been to look for us, and that they were now driving to Moscow. (He later migrated to Italy and then to the USA. We used to talk on social media about our different experiences in Russia. One day his wife found him slumped on the sofa in the living room but by the time the paramedics got there, he was dead. I wept.)

Aaron and his friends had been to the hostel looking for us and, because they could not remember what we looked like, they had beaten a few people. They only left the hostel when one of the residents telephoned the police but not before Aaron and his entourage were told that we had gone to Moscow. Apparently, they were now on their way to Moscow, headhunting us.

This telephone call did not change my plans in the slightest. I was still aiming to head to the Cameroonian Embassy to ask for an exit visa and go back to Cameroon. I had enough money to buy my own air ticket and I could not anticipate any problems. The President decided to get another train and head for Belorussia, he had a few friends there, while his associates headed to Babushkinskaya to meet with another Nigerian.

I was a bit tipsy so could not immediately go and present myself to the Cameroonian embassy, in fact Alphonse was not up for taking me to where the embassy was, so instead we headed for Kiyevskaya Metro and to the Diplomatic Corpus (a gated area reserved for diplomats) with the hope of staying the night. We stopped at the McDonald's in Kiyevskaya, which Alphonse told me was the first McDonald's store to open in Russia. During its launch in 1990, the staff and management only expected around a thousand people. Instead thirty thousand people turned up to enjoy Big Macs, making it the biggest launch of a food restaurant anywhere in the world.

Kiyevskaya McDonald's was packed with Russians (I was in post-communist Russia after all). We sat next to a Russian family but their little boy started crying. He was pointing at Alphonse saying, 'Monkey. Monkey.' Poor child. His parents tried to shut him up but that made matters worse and he cried louder. His poor mother tried calming him by saying, 'They are human, they are just black.' The child would have none of it. I didn't know what to say, I spared the family their embarrassment by pretending we didn't understand Russian.

As we were leaving, two armed officers holding a huge German

75

Shepherd stopped us—security was on high alert as Chechen militants had made their way into Moscow. I engaged in friendly banter with the officers as they examined our documents. They asked why I was in Moscow given that I was residing in Stavropol and why it was that my residence permit had not been renewed? I said it was for those very reasons we were going to the Diplomatic Corpus to see a Cameroonian consul member to rectify the residency issue. I offered the younger officer some dried fish, he politely declined and advised us to be careful. I met with this officer several times after this but he never stopped me again.

We could not stay at the Diplomatic Corpus, as we had hoped, as the house of the Cameroonian consul was full of all kind of characters; there was one guy who was so fat, it looked like he had grown into the chair, a girl who kept looking at the clock and another girl who had just been given a visa to go to America—by the way she walked and carried herself it was if she owned the world.

I remember the consul's wife very well, she looked tired, grumpy and disgruntled like one of those people in the village who would normally have witchcraft. It didn't help that she was a bit overweight. When we entered, she looked at us and did the lips and tongued gesture that most African Caribbean women do— she twisted her lips making a sound, expressing her disgust at seeing us.

Alphonse interacted with a few of the people and then we visited a British priest who lived in the same building. This was supposed to be our second place of abode but it turned out a Cameroonian, who had been adopted by the British church and who stayed at the Diplomatic corpus with father Francis, had gone into the church coffers and stolen all the tithes, which amounted to ten thousand dollars. The guy had simply disappeared into thin air. Though father Francis offered us cheese and pineapple on sticks, we were not welcome to stay at his residence (I had never dreamt of having a combination of cheese and pineapple before, it was my first time but I liked it; now it is the first thing I go for when invited to a party). I really do not think we were ever meant to be staying in any of these residencies, however, this is where Alphonse kept his loot, and this gesture would save his life later.

I was now homeless in Moscow. I had money and I knew that if it came to it, I could check into a hotel and make my way to the Cameroonian embassy the next day but Alphonse decided that we should go to Verdinha suburb and visit one of his friends called Vincent; maybe he had rooms to spare in his house.

We took the train and, looking out the window, I was awed by Moscow, at how beautiful it was. There was nothing that I saw that reminded me of home, apart from the trees, but even they looked well-groomed. Verdinha itself was amazingly beautiful, the roads were lined with diverse types of fruit trees, the flowers blossomed as if pollinated by a very special kind of bee and the houses were magnificent as we walked along. The only other place I had seen with such immense beauty was in Wales, when I was doing my Access Certificate (Sociology, Psychology and Law), at Coleg Glan Hafren in Cardiff, and we went on a college trip to Gregynog and stayed in a castle; my God that place was so beautiful, it satisfied my thoughts and dreams of what heaven would look like. Verdinha was like that— it's no wonder Mikhail Gorbachev chose it as a place to have his dacha.

Vincent had a well-decorated two-bedroom flat, which was quiet in the day but housed around eight people at night. We were told we could stay for a month for a small rent of one hundred dollars each. Vincent had been in Moscow for a long time and spoke Russian but not as well as me. I was happy to stay at Vincent's, this meant I had ample time to return to the Cameroonian embassy and arrange my return trip.

I did not need a Moscow underground map as Alphonse was with me. Alphonse had tried to persuade me to stay in Moscow, he said we formed a formidable team and had the potential to become businessmen and eventual millionaires. The idea was fine—I had made one thousand dollars after a couple of hours of translation—but I had already made up my mind about going back to Cameroon. On a personal level my heart was burdened, I was having an introspection. I would never see Anna again and, in my haste, I had left behind my small diary, which contained information including address and telephone numbers of Natalia both in Sochi and in York in the United Kingdom where she worked as an au pair. I had also left Lola heartbroken—and that kiss with Nadia was the best I had ever had. I had just disappeared from their lives, from their worlds.

Central Moscow was not as heavily policed as I had anticipated and we were not stopped at any point on our way to the embassy. The embassy itself was not heavily guarded and had just two officers in a small cubicle there to greet us. One of them was busy smoking a cigarette, the other had both hands on his gun as he paced up and down slowly; he looked homesick. I noticed a black and white cat on the wall. An ill omen I thought. I pressed the doorbell and within a few seconds the door was opened. I wasn't surprised not to be greeted in Russian but I was pissed off by the fact that the gentleman who opened the door simply assumed we spoke French.

Alphonse stayed outside and smoked a cigarette. As I walked up the stairs, I contemplated the fate of southern Cameroon's English-speaking Cameroonians; it seems we are obligated to speak French whereas French Cameroonians couldn't be bothered to speak English. The reception area was full of people with different problems. I gathered, from their conversations, that some of them had been coming to the embassy for almost a month. Everyone looked depressed. There was an imposing picture of the President of Cameroon, His Excellency Paul Biya, he had been on that wall since 1982, yet his campaign slogan for the 2018 election was 'It's Time for Change'. No matter how you positioned yourself, the imposing gaze of the president followed you. It reminded me of George Orwell's *1984*—Biya is the epitome of Big Brother.

After what seemed like hours, a small man came out of the room and, without saying a word, handed me a piece of paper. Written in French was: name, date of birth, place of birth and reason for visiting the embassy. I filled the form in and stated my reasons in bold letters, 'I would like an exit visa to return to Cameroon.' I had to state this in French due to conformity and all that. I added, 'I have money to pay for my ticket.' The cost of the ticket was four hundred dollars on the Russian airline, Aeroflot.

The longer I waited in that room, the more depressed I got. There was one guy who had been beaten by skinheads in a place called Padorlski. Everyone knew about Padorlski. Many have gone there but only a few have returned. There was another guy whose brother was in a hospital in Dynamo—skinheads had also attacked him—and another guy had had his money stolen. There were a few who were homeless and looked skeletal; their stories were gruesome.

There was one Bakossi boy who looked like a ghost, when he walked it was as if his clothes were still in the cupboard. He had growths all over his body and his face looked like he had a fungal infection, scurvy or beriberi, for he had been in a Russian prison for two years for drug dealing. He looked finished. His case was even worse because while he was in prison his savings from dealing, around five thousand dollars, had been taken by his girlfriend who was now in Germany.

The imposing picture of the president had changed: he wasn't smiling, but instead looked slightly annoyed. His left eye faced three o'clock, his right faced nine o'clock. One by one we were called into the office, I was given an official appointment for the following week. I was happy, I was going home and I was going to face my father's family head on.

Alphonse told me about one Cameroonian girl he dated but unfortunately for him, the girl's boyfriend was a professional rugby player and had a black belt in Taekwondo. It was one of those forbidden love stories that turned out to be unrequited love. It cost

79

Alphonse a floor space at the hostel as the boyfriend issued a fatwa on Alphonse. As we took the train to Verdinha, all I could see were the faces of those I had just met at the embassy that were pale and gaunt; Russia had taken its toll. I missed my village.

*

I remembered how Moki Monyama and I use to go hunting for rat moles. We never caught any despite all the planning that went into it—the rat moles always out-smarted us until Monyama learned how to make box traps. I remembered my friends Big Devil and Victor (we nicknamed him Mephistopheles), and Moses aka Likume—now a priest according to the Catholic order. I remembered Aloga my nephew (I have a strong belief he will follow my footsteps). I remembered my little sister Queenta. I missed them all.

I remembered Aunty Enanga, Mephisto's mother, how she would chastise me for stealing apples from her tree. I remembered Aunty Enanga Pa Takesh, a woman of fortitude. I remembered how Moki Peter and I invaded the farm grounds of our secondary school, in Bokwango, stealing haricot beans (that evening I had corn chaff). Peter is now the Head of Police and fighting against Boko Haram in the north and he reminds me of this incident every time we talk. He says he will sue me for the risk I put him through! The worst part is he didn't even taste the food I cooked that was so good I ate all of it.

Life for us was simple. Our parents had farms and farming was second nature to us. As children our favourite pastimes were sitting on car bonnets and sliding down the hillside. It's amazing that no one died as it was a long fall to the bottom into namonge, a small stream that was fed by the mountain. Another pastime was stealing sugar cane and pineapples from Mola Mongambe's farm. We used catapults to chase the ezruli zrulis (sun bird) and other small birds. The Njohs had a fence made up of hibiscus flowers, which attracted all kinds of birds that were drawn to sucking nectar. We followed the birds and tasted the sweet juice of hibiscus nectar.

By the time I was in upper sixth form a mysterious ailment had struck the village and the men started dying one by one. There was not a week that went by without another man dying. Most of the deaths were blamed on witchcraft. I could see my mother making my favourite food, ekwang, her eyes red, filled with smoke, probably using mangrove roots my sister Elizabeth had brought from Tiko. Though seated, she was bending forward as she prepared the food. There is a lot of artistry that goes into making this dish. First you go to the farm and gather some cocoyams, and then you peel and grate them. Most women in the village have no fingernails because they lose them in the process of cooking this meal. It's a painstakingly slow process.

Once the coco yams are grated, she will arrange them in a soft portion of coco leaves that she gathered from the back of the house. She will then align into a pot in a circular pattern allowing a hole in the middle, then you add njanga (crayfish), bonga (dried fish), stuck fish (for posh people), a dash of palm oil and some Maggi cubes. Then she will spend an age making sure the food was cooking at the right pace, increasing and lowering the heat by adding or removing firewood. There will be continued tasting and adding of different ingredients; this process will continue for two to three hours until the food is cooked. Once cooked, if you so wish, you can pan fry some extra palm oil and pour it onto the cooked kwang. This is food for the gods I tell you. The best part of ekwang is what we call wekoka (left overs), which forms part of our breakfast.

I remember once my eldest sister, Elizabeth—for some reason I had skived off from school—decided to give me a bit of home education. She was going to teach me some English idioms such as 'The devil makes work for idle hands'. It was like she was forcing water out of a rock; the idiom did not make any sense to me. Instead of paying attention, my mind was somewhere else. She said, repeating herself, 'The devil makes work for idle hands.' I was getting bored and not paying any attention. I decided to take my brother's bicycle for a ride, I had never ridden before and as soon as I jumped on the bicycle, I started shaking and could not balance or control myself. I went down

*the road shaking and eventually I bumped into Mbamba Limunga,
knocking her over. Mbamba Limunga screamed and cursed saying I
was the child of the devil, she slapped and kicked me with all the force
she could muster. She left the bike where it landed and dragged me
home, my sister had seen the incident as it unfolded and was pissing
herself with laughter.*

*When Mbamba reached the house, my sister gave me two slaps just
to assure Mbamba Limunga that she didn't condone my action. As
soon as Mbamba left, after a series of verbal abuses, tirades and rants,
my sister burst out laughing and said, 'You see, I told you the devil
makes work for idle hands.' I can't ride a bike to this day.*

*

The embassy was packed, the imposing photograph of the
President of Cameroon was still on on the wall, the picture was
even more frightening as some disgruntled visitor had decided to
paint over his eyes, making him blind. Metaphorical, I thought.
Name after name was called. Time had stopped. I got into the
embassy at 10.30 in the morning but I was only seen at 2.30 in the
afternoon. Again, our conversation was all in French.

Questions were fired at me, 'What have you been doing in
Russia? How long have you been in Russia? You said you were
born in Cameroon, yes? What is your mother's name? Where does
your mother work? What is your father's name? Where does your
father work? Have you been tested for AIDS? Are you a student?'
and on and on. I was asked all kinds of questions before being told
to wait again in reception.

*

*I was in my favourite Apostolic Church in Small Soppo Buea. After
A-levels in 1995 I joined the Apostolic church; most of the
congregation was Ibiobio and Ibo Nigerians, apart from Pastor Jacob.*

Pastor Jacob was a wonderful preacher. When he preached the gospel you felt like God was talking directly to you. The church was always packed when Pastor Jacob was preaching, he would quote verses from the Bible as if he had written them himself and, like Froy in Sochi, Pastor Jacob enjoyed the book of Daniel, especially the parable of the fat and the skinny cows and the prophecies of Daniel on Nebuchadnezzar.

I am not sure how he managed to find out I had tried kissing Enjema behind the church, but he chastised me for it. Imagine my surprise when Pastor Jacob was stripped from his pastoral duties after 'the spirit' revealed to one of the other pastors that Pastor Jacob had been having an affair with his wife and had got two members of the congregation pregnant. I took it to heart because I had a crush on one of the girls he impregnated. Pastor Jacob became an outcast. He was just an ordinary person who had memorised the Bible.

One of the reasons I went to this church was because of the music; they played beautiful Nigerian songs that had been adapted for the church. In my dream I could hear one of my favourite songs playing, 'Onye Chicca Jehovah', which was accompanied by the most beautiful drum beats. In my dream, I had transformed myself into an Ibo Nigerian and was dancing in my sleep. When the music stopped, I walked up the road towards my mother's house. I couldn't recognise a single thing. I was standing outside the house, it was quiet, and I could hear crickets chirping. I am sure I heard an owl and a toad was staring at me as if saying, 'You are in the wrong place.' I quickly returned to the house as an owl is an ill omen.

*

I was called back into the office and was asked by a member of the embassy's staff to hand over my passport. Ever since Stavropol, where I had slightly defaced my passport, I had the habit of carrying a laminated photocopy, which I handed to the staff. He looked at my picture then looked at me. He went through all the pages and asked if I had my birth certificate? I had not foreseen the outcome of his enquiries. After a few minutes of looking at my passport and looking back at me, he apologised and said that there was no way they could ascertain whether I was a Cameroonian. He proceeded to explain that a lot of Nigerians had obtained Cameroonian passports to come to Russia and that my French sounded more like a Nigerian who had been living in Kumba. He kept the photocopy of my passport and asked me to leave the embassy. I had been labelled a 'Boy boy'—one of those young children brought into Cameroon by unscrupulous Nigerian businessmen, to work endlessly as child slaves. Not only was I rejected by my paternal kinsmen, the gods had conspired to ensure I was rejected by my own country. I felt suicidal. I had to activate my backup plan.

During the first two nights of staying at Vincent's house, he had showed us a collection of passports that he was selling, which he had obtained from the black market. He had Zimbabwean, South African, Togolese, Canadian and a few Cameroonian passports (the Cameroonian passport was the cheapest, retailing for only twenty dollars, the Zimbabwean and South African sold for five hundred dollars while the American and Canadian retailed for up to one thousand dollars).

Vincent also told me about a voluntary repatriation programme run by the United Nations; he had given me the address and was convinced I would be a perfect candidate. The following day after breakfast, I made my way to a branch of the United Nations. Imagine my relief when I was told they did have a voluntary repatriation programme, but the only prerequisite was that one had to have been living in Russia for two years' minimum. I pleaded with the officer, telling him I was in the position to buy my own ticket and all I wanted was help with an exit visa; I wanted to go back home. There was no way I could have stayed or survived another winter in Russia. I pleaded with the guy until he allowed me to fill in the paperwork. I think he liked the fact that I had put effort into learning the language.

Once I had completed the questionnaire, I handed it over to the guy and sat comfortably on the huge sofa that occupied the reception area. The office smelled fresh and was well ventilated. The summer sun was hitting Moscow. When I had first arrived in Moscow, I never thought someone could wear a sleeveless top but today I took off my jacket and relaxed. There was a French flag, an American flag, an English flag and a Russian flag; they even had a Canadian flag but there was no Cameroonian flag. As I sank into the soft leather chair, my mind started drifting. How wonderful it would be to be born in one of those countries where you can just up and go, a country where your passport had the royal seal of approval. I smiled. I thought of Natalia, my first wife in Sochi, who was now somewhere in York; I thought of Anna; I thought of Lola and the wife of the nightclub owner I had a brief fling with before her husband found out. I knew I would never see them again.

*

A few weeks after Meki had been bitten by the snake he simply disappeared. At first, I just assumed he had gone to visit his mother, something he usually did. However, as the days passed, I became increasingly worried as Meki was nowhere to be found. I searched the neighbourhood, I visited Meki's parents and Victor aka Mephistopheles told me one evening that maybe Meki had been eaten by the new Nigerian couple who had moved into the compound of the Mosimas next door to Aunty Ndinge. They looked at me suspiciously when I knocked on their door to ask if they'd seen my dog. Victor laughed when I told him how astonished Mr Obassi was when I asked if he'd seen my dog, and told me he was joking.

One afternoon I heard a little scratch on my bedroom door, when I opened it Meki was standing there looking gaunt and extremely pale, his eyes red as if he had been crying. On closer inspection I realised he only had three legs and couldn't stand up straight. He had wandered off on his own into the forest and his right hind leg had been caught in a snare. I felt so sorry for Meki, he must have barked my name into the trees, hoping they would carry his tears to me. Meki had no option but to stay with the snare until the wire cut through the rotten bone. I cried when I saw Meki who looked at me accusingly. I had abandoned him, I didn't make any effort to look for him.

When I woke up in the morning, Meki's stiff body was against my door. The last thing Meki did, even close to death, was to protect me. I didn't know what to do, I woke my mum up telling her Meki was dead.

'What do you want to me to do?' she said. 'Go bury the dog.' She tapped me gently on the shoulder before going back to sleep. I cried. I dragged Meki's body to the back of the compound and dug a shallow grave and buried Meki. On top of his grave I planted some garden eggs. As Meki dissolved into the ground he fermented the soil and the fruit tree blossomed. I vowed never to have any more pets.

*

The sofa at the United Nations had sucked me into a perfect place. I had fallen into a deep slumber and was snoring loudly. When I woke up, the official sat on the other side of the sofa was laughing. He said I had been talking in my sleep and asked who Meki was and why I had been crying. He then told me I had qualified for the repatriation programme and that I should bring my passport to their office the next day; the United Nations was going to buy my ticket and arrange a pickup point. As if this was not enough, the United Nations was going to give me a two thousand dollars allowance for a business start-up in Cameroon. What a grand gesture I thought.

That evening I told Vincent I was no longer interested in buying the Zimbabwean passport as I had qualified for a free repatriation. Alphonse tried talking me out of it but my mind was made up. Russia was not for me. I was not mentally prepared, I was not strong enough to be dealing with the weather and the skinheads— I wanted to go back home. I was not streetwise, not at all, this scam was not for me. Reluctantly Alphonse resigned himself to the fact that I was going back home.

I stayed awake that night. I could even hear Vincent having intercourse with Maria, his girlfriend, in the other room because the walls were very thin. That morning I was the first to use the bathroom, and as I brushed my teeth, I looked at my reflection and smiled. I was going to kill the spiders that nested on the far corner of the sink, but when I reached to slap them with my shoe I realised they were mating and I could not bring myself to interrupt their orgasmic phantasmagoria.

In the kitchen I made the Russian breakfast of two slices of brown bread, multiple slices of ham, two boiled eggs and tea. I wore my blue jeans, white Nike trainers, a Nike T-shirt, a Chicago Bulls baseball cap, collected my passport and left Verdinha for the offices of the United Nations. The sun had already risen over the horizon and as I got on the train, I remembered the last kind gesture I did for my mother when I had cleared a field and planted her around two hundred yam tubers. I wondered how the harvest was or if they were still there or if some food thieves had stolen them.

I got to the United Nations premises so early their offices were not yet open. When they finally did, I noticed there was a new receptionist who greeted me politely and asked for my name. Mish, as he was called, spoke in English with an American accent. At this stage I still loved meeting and talking to Americans. Expecting him to say American, I politely asked where he was from. He said he was Russian but had studied English and medicine for three years in America. Our conversation fluctuated between Russian and English and I told him I had uncles in America, in Minnesota. He took my passport and retired to another room. He was there for what seemed like an age. When he came back, he looked gloomy, the smile had gone from his face, and avoided my gaze. He said, 'Sorry Mr Charles, we are in no position to help you. Unfortunately the free repatriation programme has been stopped.'

He went on to explain that the United Nations had to cancel the project after it had lost close to fifty thousand dollars. It turned out many Cameroonians and Nigerians had heard about this project and had contacted the United Nations for free repatriation, the UN had issued each of the people who wanted free repatriation with two thousand dollars, however, once they received the money, no one turned up at Sheremetyevo airport for repatriation. Countless empty flights returned to Cameroon. I pleaded with Mish, I said I would go and pack my belongings and would stay at the office till they were ready to repatriate me, that I did not want the two thousand dollars and wouldn't mind if I was going to be put on an aeroplane in chains. I wanted to go home. I pleaded with him until his manager came out of his own office, then I pleaded with him, however the decision had been made and the free repatriation had been stopped. I did not know whether to laugh or cry. I was a 'Boy boy'; manmade laws, borders and greed were conspiring against me, ensuring I was lost and abandoned forever in a country where I had no name, no face, no audience, where no one knew me. I was broken.

In my reverie I was in Cameroon, only a thin thread helped me cling onto life. I felt abandoned by my ancestors; I hated my father's family even more. No way was I going to spend another winter in Russia. It took me an age to get back to the Verdinha, where I placed my mat in the corner of the living room and fell into a deep sleep, with my eyes open.

After a day of negotiation with Vincent, I bought the Zimbabwean passport for a reduced price of three hundred and fifty dollars. I had now spent a total of four hundred and fifty dollars, three hundred and fifty for my newly acquired passport and one hundred dollars for my rent. Vincent gave me a rundown of which countries I could travel to, using the Zimbabwean passport, which included Germany, Canada and the United Kingdom. I was a bit happier. I had secured a small investment, and I could now try and travel as far as Zimbabwe and then navigate my way to Cameroon.

The poison that was building, the bile that was forming inside of me, was far more dangerous than that of a black mamba, for the inside of my mouth, gums, teeth, lips were now black in contrast to my brown skin. Outside I was full of smiles but a thunder raged inside of me. Even today, when I laugh, it is loud. I have now removed the garments of an outcast, but the laughter remains. I was heading to Zimbabwe and would struggle until I reached Cameroon, even if it meant becoming a guerrilla along the way. I had read about the Mau Mau and their night raids. I would then enter the village at night and, incognito, initiate my plan. Who would know? There was no CCTV; it would be blamed on witchcraft. We drank beer and ate salted fish, while all these ideas played out in my mind.

Once he had collected his rent for the month, Vincent became restless; he would not stay long in the house and when he was in the house, he was on the house telephone, speaking so quietly that he was on the point of whispering. He was in and out, his behaviour erratic. Vincent reminded me of the Duaine, who escaped with ten thousand dollars of student fees in Stavropol.

It was no surprise when in the early hours of the morning when Vincent was not home there was a knock on the door. I opened the door to six police officers, dressed in full riot gear, with guns and dogs. They went into every room and brought everyone into the living room. They said we must gather our things and leave. This was one of those days my Russian did not help. They were not aggressive and they didn't search the house, our bags or anything, they simply wanted us to move out as the house had been rented out to someone else. I knew it. Moscow was a dog eat dog world. These guys were police officers but they were also Vincent's friends. Vincent had collected eight hundred dollars from the eight of us and then proceeded to rent the house out to other people. The police officers were simply doing his dirty work.

Chapter 10

Alphonse gave me the telephone number of a businessman called Tigran who he had met at a café in south west Moscow. The man had approached Alphonse and invited him to be his drug mule and Alphonse had agreed. We knew this was the first step to our first scam in Moscow, but what we didn't know was that the meeting would be the first time one would be pistol-whipped and taken hostage.

I called Tigran and we arranged a meeting. At this point I only had around one hundred dollars left, which meant I didn't have any other choice but to go along with Alphonse's plans. What was the worst that could happen? Get caught? Killed? I knew I needed an exit visa, for this I needed money and I needed a permanent place to stay. What better way to make some quick money, than get an exit visa and vamoose to Zimbabwe?

We met Tigran at the underground station in Tanganskaya where the yellow and the brown lines meet. Tigran did not approach us but Alphonse had noticed him in the centre of the platform, he was wearing a long, greyish woollen jacket. He was well built and from the way his shoulders bulged, you could tell he was a gym addict. We followed him at a distance; the worst combination in Russia, especially in a group, is that of a dark-haired Russian and a dark-skinned African; this would send police signals. Black-haired Russians have it bad in Russia, especially in Moscow. I picked up a few extremely rude words that were standard in conversation among Russians. For those who were dark-skinned and recognised as being from Africa or 'The Dark Continent', we were simply obieziany (monkey). For the dark-haired Russians, Armenians, Georgians, Tartars, it was all yobany urod (which translates to 'fucking bastards'). My sixth sense did not kick in and even though the paintings on the Moscow underground shook their heads we ignored their warnings.

Once out of the station, we followed Tigran but still kept our distance until he stopped at a red Niva. He looked at us for a few seconds before opening the door and sitting in the passenger side. We crossed over the road and jumped into the back. Curiously he didn't say a single word, a few minutes later, another extremely well-built, dark-haired gentleman arrived wearing black trousers, a white shirt and a brown leather jacket. He looked extremely smart and was carrying a man bag under his arm. When he got into the car, he stank of chewing tobacco.

Alphonse turned to me and said, 'We're in the money.' The same phrase that The President used when we had a successful mission with Arban and his friends in Stavropol. Tigran drove us to a block of flats. The flats were stained with age and neglect. There was a babushka selling semechki (dried or smoked pumpkin seeds), two drunken diedushki arguing on the lavuchka (a bench outside the entrance to their apartment which was very common in most Russian apartments) and some teenagers doing parkour, using goal posts and swinging from end to end.

As we drove further into the area it opened up into beautiful, low terraced private housing surrounded by small trees and roses. Tigran dropped into first gear and came to a stop outside one of the houses. The path to the house had plenty of fresh potted plants including one flower that looked like hibiscus. Black and white slabs of tiles formed the path leading to the front of the house. It reminded me of the carpet at my aunt's house that I used to clean day and night before Mola got home from work. Tigran opened the door and let Alphonse out, the other guy whose name was Shant, was fiddling with a set of keys. We walked behind Tigran as he ushered us into the house and the sweet aroma of homemade food greeted us. They had a giant television, books, and beautiful rugs on the wall. The house was small from the outside but quite big on the inside.

Shant said, 'So guys, how are you?'

Alphonse and I replied, 'We're good'.

He nodded and said, 'Good. Let us do business.'

He placed a large bag of cocaine on the table, unfiltered. He then brought a series of small bags and told us the small bags retailed for twenty-five roubles each. He was excited, finally they'd found their own mules. Despite the problems I had had with my brother, we had become very close during my last days in Cameroon, and the one piece of advice he had given me repeatedly was to avoid drugs, taking or selling them; he had warned me of the stern and lengthy imprisonment they brought. Not only that, I had watched television in Stavropol and had seen how Ibo Nigerians with Cameroonians were being chased by the Russian police, some had drowned crossing the river. I had seen that Bakossi boy at the Cameroonian embassy who had been locked up for drugs offences so there was no way I was going to start selling drugs. It was my cue then to introduce them to our own line of business.

I had given Alphonse the last of my one-hundred-dollar bills and, together with his two-hundred, we had stained them with iodine and sealed them in a package waiting for this moment. Tigran and Shant looked on in utter amazement as I explained to them the procedure. They offered us vodka and told different anecdotes, they laughed out loud, so did we. They were going to be rich they thought, we knew we were going to be rich. I asked if they had a one-hundred-dollar bill as we only dealt in one-hundred-dollar bills. Shant disappeared into a room and came out with a clean bill. I knew the routine by heart but to put Tigran and Shant at ease, Alphonse spoke and I translated.

Alphonse was an attaché to the American Embassy. Since the fall of the Berlin Wall, America had signed contracts with different agencies in Moscow to flood the Russian market with dollars in order to undermine the Russian rouble. Producing counterfeit dollars was just a matter of mixing them with good dollars and using a chemical to wash them as Alphonse was going to demonstrate. Remember, our own dollars had been stained using iodine—this is what we present as fake dollars. Everything else is a game, a game that can have tragic consequences.

I handed over the one-hundred-dollar bill from Shant and Alphonse asked for some scissors and a black carrier bag like the one we had already prepared at home, which Alphonse carried in his pocket. As I stood in front of them, Alphonse reached into his pocket and brought out two finely cut pieces of paper we had cut into dollar sizes and stained with iodine. I handed one to Tigran, who touched and smelled it in excitement, then Shant touched and smelled it before handing it back to me. With great care Alphonse placed their new one-hundred-dollar bill between our finely cut iodine papers. He then carefully placed the contents into the clean-cut black bag, sealing all the corners. When this was done, he asked if they had gloves and a syringe in the house.

'Why do you need gloves and a syringe?' Tigran asked. I proceeded to explain how dangerous the chemicals were and that Alphonse was going to be injecting them into the sealed dollars to help complete the metamorphosis. They didn't have a syringe in the house but had gloves. So Shant left the house and a few minutes later came back with a packet of syringes. Alphonse carefully removed the sealed hospital container from his pocket, which contained nothing but a common kitchen detergent, he then unsealed the syringe, which he checked with all diligence to ensure it was working fine. All these little gestures go a long way to reassure the clients that all is genuine. The longer Alphonse took with the procedure, the more curious, keen and interested Tigran and Shant became. Tigran was then asked to make space in the freezer, as the package needed three days to rest, and it also needed three doses of chemicals injected over time. Alphonse had switched their packages so they now had our three hundred dollars in the freezer whilst we had theirs.

They insisted we stay at their house, which was a bonus as we were practically homeless. For the next two days, Alphonse left the house with Tigran in the morning and came back late in the evening. He told me he never sold drugs. The first thing Tigran would do upon entering the house was to check the contents of the freezer. On the second night Tigran and Alphonse brought a girl to the house, her name was Natasha. She worked the streets in Okhotny Ryad, in central Moscow. I do not know how much Tigran had paid Natasha but she was paid.

As we walked Natasha to the train station the following day, we were stopped by two police officers. They were not interested in our documents but took more of an interest in Natasha. They hurled her into the car and that was it. Our paths never crossed again.

On the third day, the day of reckoning, the day when all would be revealed, the day of opening the package, there was a third person in the house. I cannot remember his name, but his man bag was slightly bigger than Shant's. It explained why Shant had been talking on the telephone for most of the previous evening, not in Russian but Armenian. As we sat around the table, he opened his bag and brought out a brown envelope containing ten thousand dollars. Tigran said he didn't want to be messing about, he just wanted to do one big deal and retire, and that is why he had invited his friend along. Alphonse and I were happy. I didn't realise it was going to be this easy. Soon I was going to be able to afford an exit visa.

All we had to do was bide our time and find a place where we could cut out thirty thousand dollars' worth of bills. My gosh, our box trap had a rat mole—we were in the money.

Tigran brought the package and placed it on the table. Shant had a small piece of paper in his hands, which were a bit shaky. The other guy sat at the end of the table quietly, ten thousand dollars in front of him. Alphonse asked Tigran for a bowl of warm water from the kitchen then, using his syringe, dropped a few drops of detergent into the bowl. Wearing his gloves, he slowly unwrapped the package. He then placed the one-hundred-dollar iodine-darkened bills into the bowl of water. Slowly the iodine disappeared and the dollars turned back to their original state. The eyes of the guy with the ten thousand dollars almost jumped out of their sockets. He was excited; this was magic they were witnessing. They chatted out loud, talking about how this will be their new investment branch. They asked why they'd not heard of such an advance in technology before? Alphonse spoke in English and I translated saying it was highly classified, you needed to have or know someone at the American embassy. Let me tell you, the way the iodine clears from the dollar paper, even you would be convinced of how genuine this scam was. One by one Alphonse cleaned the dollars and allowed them to dry. Once dried, they were ironed.

Shant took the dollars and studied them. The guy was very clever; he had written down the serial number of the one-hundred-dollar bill he had given us three days ago, so when he checked, his own dollar had mysteriously disappeared. He knew something was amiss but he could not fathom what. He checked the serial numbers again and again, then, with Tigran and the third guy, they adjourned to the other room. Their dialogue became loud and aggressive but they spoke Armenian. Alphonse was breathing fast, I was shaking. I thought about opening the door and running but Alphonse had read my mind and he said, 'Eric, don't do it!' Even if I had managed to open the door and started running, where would I have gone? When they came out from the room, only Tigran had a smile on his face, Shant and the other guy looked pissed off.

'Come on guys, let's go to the money exchange,' said Shant. You can imagine how relieved we were. I wondered why Shant didn't sit in the front with Tigran, instead the passenger seat was empty while Alphonse and I were squeezed in the back of the car with Shant and his friend. We arrived at Aviamotornaya station where the money exchange was but there was no sign of the car stopping.

We drove on, the road becoming narrower. Shant said, 'Would you like some nganja (cannabis)?' His eyes were red, the car smelled, Alphonse was shaking. I knew this was the day our lives here on earth would end. Eventually we came to an isolated derelict building. My heart was beating fast. I was playing with fire, I knew my hands would get burned. Shant opened his door and stepped out, throwing the last part of his nganja under the car and held the door open for me. As soon as I came out of the car, I was hit just under my jaw with the butt of a short gun. I saw stars flickering and passed out.

*

I hated school as a child because I was dumb, and I mean really dumb. My mother would walk me to the Small Soppo Catholic school but I would deliberately leave my books at home, so the teacher would then send me home to get my books – this became routine. I snapped out of the habit when one day the teacher had had enough; she used a massive ruler to hit me fifty times on my knuckles. When I showed my mother my swollen knuckles that evening and told her how I got them, she went to the back of the house and got a cane, we called Mbeti, and beat me again. This was not unusual, if your teacher or any other adult reported you to your parents, it would be worse—no investigation, just further punishment.

It was more than an hour's walk to go back home and then back to school, so instead I would go to where my mother worked. My mother is extremely good at maths and worked as an accountant for the Cameroon Development Corporation in Tole. I say accountant, just to make it sound a bit posh but she was ill paid for the job.

Instead of going home to get my books, I would visit my mother. Her friends would recognise me from a distance and I would hear them shouting, 'Sarah, your child with the big stomach is coming again.' I had a huge stomach as a child, in some quarters people even suggested that I had kwashiorkor, which was a life-threatening and debilitating form of malnutrition caused by lack of protein in the diet. I also had permanent mucous coming down my nose. It never bothered me, but the fact that I timed my visit to my mother when she and her friends were on lunch breaks meant I was the last person they wanted to see.

One of my mum's friends, Aunty Monjowa, would say, 'Eric, I beg you, wipe your nose.' I would use the back of my hand to clean my nose, however this only made matters worse as it meant I smeared the mucous all over my mouth. This made the women eating their lunch nauseous and angry. They would tease my mother, 'Please take your child to the hospital, he is not well.'

I saw myself going back to school with my empty bag, the teacher chastised me and asked me to go home and get my books, instead I abandoned my bag behind the building and walked towards my mother. Only this time she was not there, Aunty Monjowa was not there to call out my mother's name, the women were not there to tell me to wipe my nose. I was a stranger. Maybe I was dying, my life was flashing past me.

*

When I woke up, I was naked and tied to a chair, back to back with Alphonse, who was also naked, our clothes in a pile across the room. There was blood on the floor, my legs felt as if they were on fire. Alphonse then told me what had transpired whilst I was unconscious. Tigran and his friends had searched all our nooks and crannies, he said they knew we had tried scamming them but could not understand what had happened to their money. They could not understand how it had mysteriously vanished. They didn't realise that we had swapped bills days ago, when we had initiated the scam. The truth is if they had found their hundred dollars, I do not think I would be writing this story.

Summer was at its peak so even though we were both naked and had spent the night naked, it was not terribly cold. The following day only Tigran turned up, they had taken all the money that Alphonse had. He asked what had happened to the money Shant gave us? I swore to him Shant had made a mistake. He was confused.

He cut the ropes and watched as we dressed, he then got back into his car and drove away. My whole body was in pain. I do not know what they had done to Alphonse, and we never spoke about that incident again. He looked worse for wear. It took us ages to get to the nearest underground station. Luckily there was no one controlling the train barriers and we jumped on the train all the way to Taganskaya, where we changed to the brown line that goes around and round central Moscow. Most homeless people use the brown line to while away their days. As the train went around and around, I remembered the first time my mother banished me from the village.

*

In order to be near her place of work, my mother had decided to move into a neighbourhood called Tole, in a street called Mbo Quarter. Tole's reputation preceded her; many children from Small Soppo, my own village, were scared to attend school because of the fear of encountering children from Tole. They were wild, ill bred. For the sake of company, my mother took my nephew Collins, my baby sister Queenta, and myself, with her to Tole. Surprisingly Tole was okay but one could smell the air of poverty. Apart from one or two, all the houses were made of what we call carabot (soft wood). The rest of the area is surrounded by a vast tea plantation, which was the only employer around and exploited the workers to its fullest.

My Mother, Iya Sarah Efeti Kange, is the first child of late Mola Mosre Mo Ngwa Kange. I am not sure whether she was born in Cameroon or in Nigeria, but her mother, my grandmother, came from a place called Mevio, a few minutes from Tole. During our short stay in Tole, we enjoyed visiting the extended side of our family. I remember Njie taking us to a small stream and showing us the footprints of porcupines. It was Njie who got me interested in dogs.

All her siblings love my mother. The first time I contemplated murder was when, as a boy, my mother was involved in that ghastly motor accident caused by Patrick Agar. Seeing her in so much pain, I feared the worse. In our district most people who go to the hospital with minor illnesses do not come out alive as medical facilities are lacking. Most people who have died in the village do not get a cause of death; more often than not the popular opinion is witchcraft.

I can still see my mother with those drips and bandages, crying in excruciating pain—she didn't stand a chance. When she heard my voice, she opened her eyes and looked at me scornfully—she blamed the accident entirely on me. When I got to the house that evening, I sat outside like a chimpanzee cracking palm nuts and eating. I went into the kitchen and brought out my mother's special machete and began sharpening it. I cried, I ran my thumb on the sharpened blade, it was ready. I wrapped it in a white sheet and placed it amongst the dry wood on the mbanda, where we dry firewood, fish and meat for the rainy season. I promised myself, if my mother should die, I was going to kill Mr Agar. He wasn't hard to find as he lived next door to my mum's sister in Stone Quarter in Tole. He had been driving his car with no headlights while towing a trailer. The car had just missed my mother, but the trailer had knocked her over and the wheels had climbed over her stomach. I was going to kill him. I was around seven years old.

About a month after my mother had been discharged from hospital and was on the road to full recovery, my sister Ndinge had cooked her favourite meal, ekwang. As we sat and ate my mother said, 'Eric (when my mother calls me Eric, it simply means I have done something wrong), when you finish go pack your bag.' She was effectively exiling me from the village for my own safety.

The following morning, my sister Christie picked me up and took me to Clerks quarters. From there we got a taxi to Mile Seventeen where we then caught a crowded bus to Kumba. From Kumba, we *caught a bus via Ekondo Titi eventually arriving in Mundemba seven hours later. According to my mother's reasoning, the villagers had placed a curse on her, hence her accident and this only happened because the tales I had told about her being missing. I left the village in 1985 and only returned three years later to go to secondary school.*

*

We decided to get off in Kiyevskaya after many hours of circling Moscow. I was back to square one: no money, no fixed abode, the only item of value I had was my Zimbabwean passport. As we headed towards the main exit, we heard footsteps and loud cries coming towards us. It was a very skinny black guy. He had been attacked outside the station by skinheads and had managed to escape but they had chased him into the station. I couldn't run even if I wanted to; my legs were swollen. We looked at the guy, he was bleeding onto the platform. It was like some sort of conspiracy; the trains are always regular but today there were no trains. We had no option but to form a tripartite. About nine youths arrived on the platform carrying broken bottles, penknives and bicycle chains. When they saw one had become three, they stopped. I had no strength left and Alphonse looked haggard. They could have killed us. They wanted to kill us. A few passers-by amplified their anger by encouraging them. It was a standoff, we were only saved when a train arrived and two police officers got off and chased the skinheads out of the station. The Ghanaian, whose name was Achikere, had a swollen face and was bleeding. We waited with him until an ambulance arrived and carried him away. I am grateful I made friends with the cleaners and officers who guarded Kiyevskaya Metro—it became my hiding place after an attempted murder in Babushkinskaya. I slept rough in Kiyevskaya metro for two nights before Alphonse visited me with good news.

Chapter 11

The Babushkinskaya district is in the north-eastern part of Moscow and forms one of the hundred and twenty-five regions of Moscow. Named after the Russian aviator, Mikhail Babushkin, it was full of tall buildings when Alphonse and I moved there in the summer of 1998. Chief—who became our main sponsor—also lived there and was in the drug business along with The President's associates; the three of them shared a one-bedroom flat from where they ran their operation.

Chief was the Kingpin: he picked up his drugs between Shabolovskaya and Leninsky Prospekt in southern Moscow. Then he would spend the evening wrapping them in small foil papers before tying them in cling film; Alphonse helped him from time to time. I really admired his courage. I was too much of a chicken to even contemplate selling drugs because my brother's warning rang in my ears.

Chief's target area was along the streets around Biblioteka Imeni Lenina in central Moscow. He never strayed, and only supplied regular customers. Chief was an Ibo Nigerian. He had been brought to Kumba by a Nigerian businessman when he was just six years old and had worked with this Oga until he was seventeen, when he was allocated his own small store to sell Garri (what remains after cassava has been processed) and groundnuts. He was very creative and branched out and started selling second-hand clothes. When his Oga saw that he was thriving, he reported him to the police and customs officers who would visit him from time to time and extort bribes, mostly in the middle of the night, and at times he was threatened with deportation.

Chief started plotting against his Oga. First, he managed to bribe his way into obtaining a Cameroonian birth certificate. Once he had that, he got himself a Cameroonian passport, and was then introduced to a baron in a place called Fiango in Kumba. The baron took his documents to Yaoundé, where they obtained a Russian visa for him. Once this was in place Chief arranged with armed robbers to visit his Oga's house in the middle of the night, while the family were in bed. They stole twelve million CFA francs, the equivalent of sixteen thousand pounds. When Chief arrived in Russia, he had four million CFA francs. What a contrast to when I arrived in Moscow with just three dollars.

Chief was full of stories. I remember this one story he told about travelling from Nigeria back to Cameroon along the high seas with goods and their boat capsized, everyone went overboard, and no one was wearing lifejackets. A lot of his travelling companions died. He tried swimming but there was no land in sight—all he could see was the earth's horizon at a distance. He gave up any hope. He knew he would die. He said he saw angels waving at him; he saw different devils with Satan at the helm, all laughing and gnashing their teeth. His hands went first, then his legs. He couldn't swim and he started sinking. He said it was the first time he regretted being obese. When he woke up, he was being resuscitated by a Cameroonian Army officer somewhere in the Bakassi Peninsula (a disputed territory between the Cameroonian and Nigerian Governments). Chief returned home empty-handed. His Oga did not believe his story—instead he thought Chief had scammed him and sold the goods to another bidder (this was not uncommon).

I liked Chief; he was always smartly dressed. If you saw him, you would not think he sold drugs because he just looked like an embassy official. He had these huge black boots, a preference of the skinheads in Moscow, and always carried a man bag with him with his drugs concealed inside his belt. He was a typical Ibo man. In order to blend into the Russian society, he used bleaching creams to appear a bit white or mixed race, which was a widespread practice amongst Ibo Nigerians. It is also endemic within the Congolese community.

I liked Alphonse and Chief, but I was tired; I wanted to go to Cameroon, to home. I missed my mother; I missed her home-cooked meals. My father's family had rejected me, the Cameroonian Embassy had rejected me for not being Cameroonian enough, at the Nigerian Embassy they all looked like Mr Adewouble and the United Nations had stopped their free repatriation programme as it had been abused by my own kind. I had been held hostage, battered with the butt end of a short gun, my Cameroonian passport had been defaced and my only solace was in the fact that I was now a Zimbabwean.

During the first few mornings, I would leave Babushkinskaya and go for a walk around Moscow, visiting different coffee houses and small discount stores looking for potential clients. The summer was at its peak and I loved the hot sun on my back. I roamed around Moscow in total reverie of home, oblivious of the risk to a black man walking around unaccompanied. My only solace was in the language.

I explored the Russian Metro, the complex network of trains running deep underground, the beautiful paintings on the walls. I wondered the fate of those who toiled in constructing such a thing of beauty. I remembered Alphonse had told me that in order to keep the construction skills a secret and preventing them from falling into the hands of Western countries, after they finished constructing the Metro most of the engineers were sent to the Gulags in deep Siberia, where they toiled until their final days. Sometimes, I didn't even go looking for clients, and caught the train at Babushkinskaya station and joined the circle line at Prospekt Mira station. I just sat down and went around and around Moscow. As I sat in that train underground, I asked why had the gods placed such burden on my shoulders? From time to time my thoughts would drift to when I was a young, up-and-upcoming village wrestler.

*

For me, wrestling was about brute force and raw strength. I had plenty, and this was my conviction until I met a young boy from Bokwango village. I remember that day very well. It was a Sunday, my mother was dressed in her traditional garment and the whole village was caught up in euphoria and total merriment. Cups and antelope horns were filled with palm wine, and the chiefs of the three villages were there, including my maternal grandfather, chief Mosre Mo Gwa Kange (Dog of Dawn Kange) as he had not yet been accused of witchcraft.

The djembe played louder and louder. The way the drummers' hands caressed those drums, with such ease, such dexterity, as if their hands and the cacophony of sounds were a directive from the gods. Jude Tita aka Kebuma was there, wearing a brown suit and yellow Pierre Cardin shoes; Jude always dressed smart, he was a trendsetter straight from the school of Grand Eugene Kebei. Jude and I are not blood relatives but are spiritually connected.

Mola Maimbe was doing the elephant dance. Pa Takesh, the guy who had killed my goat, was the village champion and he took me under his wing. He had attended most of my training sessions and admired my strength. Pa Takesh sat in the corner: as the head of Obassinjom, the village juju, all kind of different rituals were taking place under his guidance. The whole village rallied behind me, they knew I was a gift from the gods. I danced around, parading myself to both the crowd and my opponents, bare-chested; I was wearing a pair of red shorts Jude had bought for me during one of his trips to Great Soppo market. We jumped and danced to the drumbeat, shaking our biceps in an attempt at intimidating our opponents. Many have forfeited their fights just by the sheer display of muscles shown by their opponents during the pre-fight rituals.

Someone touched me on my shoulders, and when I turned around, it was a guy that looked like a molikilikili (stick insect). My confidence was boosted tenfold! This guy had guts; he had the cahones to challenge me yet he was as lean as a praying mantis. I knew straight away the fight wasn't going to last. Boosted by the sight of the molikilikili, I ran around flexing my biceps. I looked at my mother who was proudly shaking her head and muttering something as she pointed towards the heavens. She repeated the same gesture as she pointed to the ground and I knew she was doing the zromelelele, something that has been handed down to us over the generations. She was thanking the heavens for blessing her with such a brave child whilst at the same time thanking our dearest departed for keeping an eye on her precious son. This incantation was normally followed by the pouring of alcohol on the ground, but she had none.

I ran towards Enjema, my childhood crush, and I blew a kiss in her direction; she shied away and hid behind her sister. I loved Enjema. One thing was certain, after my victory, the least I would be getting from Enjema was a kiss. I had dreamt so many times about kissing Enjema. I would demonstrate my strength to her and the whole village as a hunter-gatherer, my rites of passage completed.

The drums became even louder: we danced, we were in a trance, and things from another spiritual realm possessed us. I danced for two hours nonstop. I had evolved into an elephant; I was in Cameroon. The umpire blew his whistle and we withdrew to our various corners. To add to my glamorous look I had my face painted pure black with charcoal, and the liquid of some ancient root was dropped into my eyes. I looked like a sorcerer's son if ever you've seen one—my eyes red with anger. The drums played even louder. I was ready to make the molikilikili lay prostrate, to bow in my presence.

Mola Maimbe was the first to be summoned to the middle of the ring. His fight didn't last long, he used a technique called Vanga whereby you hit your opponent hard on the back of their head at the top end of the spine. Hitting them once is enough, but Maimbe hit his opponent three times and the guy had to be resuscitated. It was brutal. It turned out that this guy had impregnated Mola Maimbe's sister on a one-night-stand and had legged it.

The next person to go was Mola Pa Takesh. The aura he carried into the centre of the ring saw his opponent shaking and his fight was short-lived. After just three rounds, his opponent forfeited as he could not take the beating he was receiving. It was then the turn of Izruma, and after the sixth round, his fight was declared a draw.

Then it came to pass, the moment the whole village had been waiting for: today Eric Ngalle Charles, the son of late Oscar Ngalle Charles, was to become a man. The drums became frenzied and I could see Mola Samba, Small Mbamba, Queenta, Aloga, Moses, Njoh, Peter Moki, all jumping with excitement. I flexed my biceps and looked at the little molikilikili, who was already in the middle of the ring; I knew I was going to kill him. 'Why did he decide to place himself at such risk?' I thought to myself. Today was the day the gods had written; today was the day of his demise. Even the weaverbirds on the palm tree opposite the Vefonge household had stopped to watch. We shook hands and took a step back waiting for the final warnings and directives before the umpire's whistle.

To this day I cannot clearly say what happened; the memory has been lobotomised. One thing I am sure of is that the molikilikili from the village of Bokwango had used some serious juju and possible witchcraft on me, for as soon as the umpire blew his whistle, the molikilikili simply disappeared. The next thing I knew, my back was on the ground. I cannot remember what happened, did I close my eyes? Once I heard the whistle, I approached the molikilikili as rehearsed repeatedly but he'd disappeared right in front of my eyes; the next thing I knew, I was flat on the ground like a log, a heavy one too. Around me everything was quiet, even the weaverbirds were astonished by what they were witnessing.

The molikilikili was held high in the sky and his camp was in total jubilation, he had effectively brought down the njoku (elephant). I tried looking at where Enjema was standing but she had disappeared in shame and embarrassment for she too had brought her mother and her entire household. I looked in the direction of my mother, who had her head between her knees and her hands folded tight behind her head.

I do not know for how long I was on the ground, I begged for it to open up and swallow me. I had brought shame on the entire village. All I wanted to do was to vanish into thin air. I prayed to the gods but they had deserted me in my greatest hour of need. Dazed and confused I walked towards the crowd; they parted as if I was a plague of biblical proportion. I dreaded the thought of facing any late spectators, so instead of climbing the Wonganga hill, instead of walking past the Efange household, instead of crossing the bridge to our house, I took the back roads. I went via the local Wonganga Baptist church, I stopped and collected a few mangoes from Pa Ngeke's tree, not one but two black cats crossed the narrow road in front of me, the weaverbirds sang in chorus as if saying, 'Shame, shame, you have brought shame on the village.'

This day was going to get worse and I knew it. I walked towards Namonge—a small stream that came and went with the rain season. It was here in Namonge that I saw Mola Ngeke kissing my big sister Christina. It was here along the banks of Namonge that Monyama's box trap first caught a rat mole. I crossed Namonge, climbing the hill into Mola Mongambe's farm, I harvested a few pineapples and some sugar cane, and I also collected a few enyengenyenge (strawberries). I checked my fence traps but nothing had been caught. I then heard a noise and I saw a black mamba gliding above in a tree. I remained still as it passed. I walked past the graves of my Aunty Moliko and Aunty Christi, then Aunty Sophie must have looked through the thatched window of her kitchen and saw me for she called out, 'Ngalle, is that you?' I did not respond. Sluggishly, I walked on. Normally I would have stopped and eaten some of her kwacoco or cocki corn. Aunty Sophie's kwacoco and cocki corn can induce greed and gluttony.

I climbed the small hill, and touched the blocks of my sister's new building. I saw an agama lizard shaking its head in total disappointment. How did it know I had lost the fight? I picked up a stone and aimed it in the direction of the agama lizard and missed. It shook its head again, this time mockingly. I carried on walking until I reached our kitchen. I opened the door; the squeaky noise had become worse. First, I set down the sugar cane, then the pineapples, then placed a handful of enyengenyenge into my mouth before putting the rest into a bowl. I sat down and rested my back on the ewongo.

I could see my mother's posture, her head between her knees and her hands over her head, the silence of the drums, the little molikilikili being lifted skywards by his friends, family and teammates. Amalinze, the cat whose back never touched the ground, had been reduced to a laughing stock, reduced to a nobody by a molikilikili from Bokwango village. Enjema had disappeared into the crowd. This was the day my wrestling career ended.

That evening, before my mother returned home, I took five hundred CFA francs, the equivalent of fifty pence from her purse, I took my chewing stick (I had no toothbrush at the time) and I took my book of Swahili songs of Love and Passion. Again, not wanting to be seen by any one, instead of going past Longstreet which was just five minutes up the road, I walked downwards and climbed the WoPa Takesh hill, I went past Ngunge's house, past Lovett's house, continued climbing past Mola Yahanesse's house, past the house of the Elives (I looked and I could see Peter Kudjo and Peter Matute arguing about something, they waved at me but I carried on), past Ajax Maija ma Ngowa's stadium (don't worry about the grandiose name, it was just a small patch of ground where we played football). I followed the narrow path past the Ellison household, and I carried on walking past Borstal institute (a detention centre for part-time criminals).

Shame and pride meant I had taken the longest route ever. I carried on walking past the beautiful government building, and I could see my school on the far-left corner. The witchcraft used by the molikilikili meant I almost walked all the way to Bokwango village, his village. As the gravel met the tarred road, I saw a taxi and flagged it down. The driver looked at me suspiciously, I was loaded with sweat and was beginning to smell and had completely forgotten I still had charcoal on my face and the red liquid in my eyes that made me look devilish. The driver pointed this out as he drove off.

Normally I would go and visit my uncle Andre, my mother's brother, but I wasn't in the mood now. Uncle Andre's children are my brothers and sisters. Uncle Andre, being a headmaster, was a strict disciplinarian, he would have enquired as to the impromptu visit. Instead, I travelled to Tiko.

My sister and her husband, Mola Paddy. They were always pleased to see me because big sister Elizabeth was effectively my mother and Mr Paddy my father. They accepted my gifts of pineapples, mangoes and enyengenyenge. I was here on a self-imposed exile for a month. They never enquired as to my mysterious appearance. My sister was happy as my visit meant she or her husband did not have to rush home after work to cook for Evenye or Fonta, their two young children. These chores were now my calling.

*

It was during one of such tours of the Moscow underground, lost in the deepest of thoughts, that I decided to go to a student hostel in a place called Pechatniki—one of the twelve regions in the southeastern area of Moscow. I had heard a lot about Pechatniki, which was painted as being worse than the bottom of hell by those who have been there. I wasn't just apprehensive—I was terrified. But the thought and knowledge that I was going to meet one of my all-time heroes spurred me on.

Meeting with Ifeoma the Great had an overwhelming pull and blinded me to all the treachery I had heard about Pechatniki. He was our all-time hero, a footballing demigod. All the youth across the south-west of Cameroon knew Ifeoma the Great and worshipped the ground he walked upon. One of the best periods of my childhood was spent in Mundemba in Ndian Division, amongst the Barondo people, (in my opinion, the Barondo people are the politest in the world, their greeting ritual can send someone bananas) and it was here that I first came across Ifeoma the Great with my little sister Queenta and my nephew Collins.

Ifeoma the Great was a far better footballer than Ronaldo or Lionel Messi. All the little flicks and kicks those guys are doing today, Ifeoma the Great was perfecting in the late 1980s. He played for Ndian Rivers, the local team in Mundemba, and my nephew, my little sister and I would stay up all night waiting for the return of Ndian Rivers from their away games. More importantly we awaited the return of Ifeoma the Great. We followed the results by listening to one of the greatest radio journalists in Cameroon, Papa Zakarinko, who was so good at radio commentaries that when people started having television sets in the villages, they still would rather listen to his commentaries on radio. I am sure my very good friend Abel Akara Ticha (head of communications at the African branch of the United Nations) honed his skills listening to Zakarinko. I didn't have any problems at the entrance of the hostel; I had parliaments (Russian cigarettes) that I offered the guards, who were completely different to the ones in Stavropol. They had their guns in plain view—Kalashnikovs that hung on the wall. There were three guards in total, all wearing military camouflage: one who checked documents, one on the side of the window and another at the back. Later, when I came to live in Pechatniki, I found out why it had been coined hell on earth. I noticed that the guard at the back never spoke; he looked like a bulldog with teeth ready to bite one's head off. The guards in Stavropol only had batons on display; maybe they hid their guns, and were most of the time tipsy on homemade vodka.

I handed them my Zimbabwean passport and they enquired as to my reasons for visiting Pechatniki. I engaged with them in Russian. We chatted briefly before they handed back my passport. No questions were asked about my lack of visa or residency permit. I was tempted to use the lift to the third floor because I had never been in a lift before. We had a lift in Stavropol but no one used it; the sound it made was as if the engineers who built it were pushing from underneath.

As I walked the corridors of the third floor in Pechatniki, the smell of Cameroonian pepper soup became more and more invasive. Curiously, all the doors were locked and the silence was intrusive. You see, most of the people who lived on the third floor in Pechatniki were illegal. At the far end of the balcony I saw a guy who introduced himself as Abraham Fenton. I asked if he was related to Cynthia Fenton? As luck would have it, he was.

*

Cynthia and I attended high school in Molyko Buea together. I was in upper sixth whilst she was in lower sixth. We had a wonderfully platonic relationship. The Fentons lived in New Layout, they knew my sister Elizabeth, Mr Paddy her husband and their children, they knew my mother, and they knew Collins and Queenta. Abraham had heard about me but we had never met. When I was in the Upper Sixth Form I used to teach history, economics and literature to Form Five students. I could deconstruct classics such as The Canterbury Tales, Silas Marner: The Weaver of Raveloe *and* The Thirty-Nine Steps *as well as the likes of Ola Rotimi, Chinua Achebe, Wole Sonyinka, Nguggi Wa Thiongo. They were birds, I was a butterfly, flapping, catching up with them. My reputation had grown around New Layout and I had my small group of followers.*

*

Abraham and I became friends and along with Ifeoma the Great, Jerome and Yvan, were my pillars.

We all lamented when Abraham never returned to the hostel from the killer shift lifting boxes at the market in Komsomolskaya; he had been followed by immigration officials and stopped outside the hostel and taken to a detention centre where he was repatriated to Cameroon. Today, Abraham is an American citizen after his wife got a Green Card and later invited him over. Abraham, in fact, knows Mola Mbua; the juju man, the quack, the charlatan who subjected me to those nights at New Layout children's graveyard.

I asked if he knew Ifeoma the Great and if indeed Ifeoma the Great was in the hostel. We walked towards the end of the hallway and Abraham knocked on a door, which was opened by a French lady. The smell of cow foot pepper soup almost knocked me out. There were four other guys in the room besides the French lady, who turned out to be the author of the enticing aroma. I bought two bowls, one for me and one for Abraham. The cook had established herself on the third floor. The pepper soup came with a big bowl of pounded cocoyam, which we call fufu. A very suitable food for the winter: heavy and warm. No one cared about calorie intake at the time and she was making a mint. Almost everyone who worked those killer shifts at Komsomolskaya market came to visit her for some food and alcohol.

Abraham said, 'Go ahead then Ngalle, tell us about Ifeoma the Great.' I narrated our childhood experience in Mundemba, how we waited for Ifeoma the Great to return from his heroics, how he was regarded as a demi-footballing-god. I was serenading Ifeoma the Great with all kinds of praises without knowing he was sat next to me all the time in a nostalgic repose. After around a half-hour of singing Ifeoma the Great's praises, he stood up, introduced himself and gave me the biggest hug ever. I felt I had found my big brother again, and I was slightly embarrassed. Ifeoma the Great was the most down to earth individual; here I was shaking hands with someone we had considered to be a god. He looked slightly shorter than I had expected. I wished my little sister Queenta and my nephew Collins were here to witness this moment.

I bought Ifeoma the Great a bowl of pounded fufu and pepper soup. I bought drinks for everyone in the room. It was great and we reminisced. The last time I had seen Ifeoma the Great was at a bar restaurant back home: I was selling puff puff, when I glanced over and saw Ifeoma the Great kissing Kongwe—one of the twins who lived opposite our house in Mundemba. We spoke about my friend and classmate Orume Nelson Baser and my childhood came flooding back. Little did I know that this little display of one hundred roubles would set a template for what was to come. Little did I know that my reputation was already in the hostel as a fluent Russian speaker. I was in demand. I stayed at the hostel until late in the evening and as I was about to leave for Babushkinskaya, two guys called Essilor and Barthelemy approached and asked if they could meet me at Pechatniki station the next day as they had a business proposal for me.

I have heard several versions of this incident, from people who were not there, people who were never witnesses. This, however, is what happened: I was there, I actively took part, and I was with Alphonse when he was taken hostage. Alphonse was with me when these men entered our house and used the wooden legs of a broken chair to batter us. Alphonse saw the guy dressed in full military uniform shouting at onlookers to stop me whilst pointing his gun in my direction.

This is my confession.

I never told Chief or Alphonse that I had met Essilor and Barthelemy at Pechatniki and that they had proposed a business idea to me. I never told Alphonse or Chief that I had met a Bakossi guy called Francis and that Francis and I had been going to Aviamotornaya, at least two or three times, to visit his girlfriend. It was during one such stay-over in Aviamotornaya that, in a drunken stupor, I mistakenly gave Francis our house telephone number in Babushkinskaya. I had broken the cardinal rule and it came back to hurt us.

When I left the house that morning, I told Alphonse and Chief I was going to meet with a potential business client. They were happy I had met clients but shocked as to how far I had spread my tentacles. I didn't follow my routine: I caught the train at Sviblova and met Barthelemy and Essilor at Pechatniki station. They didn't have money for the connecting trip to Sevastopolskaya, but it wasn't a problem for me, and I paid for their tickets. They couldn't speak an inch of Russian, not even simple *Da* or *Niet*, to save their lives. Together we travelled to southern Moscow to a place called Sevastopolskaya.

I dreaded going to Sevastopol. The kind of news coming out from there meant we were putting our lives at risk. One of the rumours was that a Black Ghanaian who had fallen asleep on the train found himself in Sevastopolskaya on the last train. He was found dead with a bullet wound in his head. The investigation showed he was shot with a standard issue police rifle. No one was ever charged or arrested for this. The argument was that the guns had been smuggled into Moscow by an Estonian dissident.

Sevatopolskaya market was in full flow—it was buzzing—and no one noticed the three black men navigating their way through the crowd. There were no police officers in sight and no one bothered us. It looked like we were in Great Soppo market; everyone was either buying or selling. We came to a stop at a huge liquor store where Barthelemy introduced me to an Armenian man.

I cannot remember this guy's name but he took us to the back of his store as they had been expecting us. He presented us with an assortment of goat's cheese, some mixed cold beef and glasses of vodka. Then he said, 'Okay guys, how can I help you?' This was my cue. Barthelemy and Essilor didn't have a clue what I was going on about, I told him I worked as a translator for an American businessman who was involved in buying and selling fake dollars. This part of the process was by now routine to me. I didn't even have to think about it, it just flowed. Essilor and Barthelemy would, from time to time, interrupt the conversation, as they couldn't understand Russian. As the conversation went on, I realised a deal was impending, this guy bought everything I was telling him, and he was ready to invest.

It's not a case of my heart being split between Essilor and Barthelemy. I knew that I would not be involving them in the deal. I could not betray Alphonse and Chief. I was the translator, I had the yam and the knife; I could cut any way I saw fit. I arranged to come back and see the client the next day to carry out a demonstration. Again, following the routine, I told him the minimum amount required so that both parties would make money was five thousand dollars. He was quite happy when I told him America was flooding the Russian market with dollars.

As we left the market, I told Essilor and Barthelemy that the client had said we should come back in a fortnight's time. I promised them I would sponsor the deal, that I just needed time to gather materials. We stopped at a café and drank a few more vodkas. They were excited that they had someone to sponsor their deal, while I was planning my flight.

Chapter 12

Two weeks had passed since we succeeded in scamming the businessmen from Sevastopolskaya out of five thousand dollars. Alphonse and I split three thousand dollars between us and gave Chief two thousand dollars, since he was the main investor. Again, the conversation was of me staying in Moscow to do some more transactions but I was determined to leave Russia. I wanted to trek across Zimbabwe and back to Cameroon. My mind was made up.

In my briefcase I had one-hundred-dollar bills in different envelopes for my mother and my sister while for my nieces and nephews, I had arranged ten, ten-dollar bills in different envelopes with their names on. On my way to the airport in the morning I planned to stop at the post office and send the money to Cameroon. I even had fifty dollars for my girlfriend Beatrice, who I loved, and who my mother loved even more. I had called Beatrice the evening before and told her I was leaving Russia the following day. This was the later part of summer 1998.

That evening, after returning from his daily routine on the streets of Moscow, Chief cooked egussi soup and pounded yam. We had invited Vincent to the house and he would accompany us to the airport. I had bought some new clothes, all brand names, and a nice pair of Adidas trainers. As we sat enjoying the food and drinks, the house phone rang once and stopped, it rang again and stopped; the third time it rang I picked it up and answered, 'Yes?'

The voice on the other side said, 'Is Eric home?' I quietly placed the phone down.

The next thing we knew, there were multiple knocks on the door and the bell was ringing nonstop. When Alphonse tried peeping through the spyhole he discovered it had been taped up.

I looked through the window and saw there were cars parked behind the house. Then my name was called out three times, 'Erico! Erico! Erico!' Only a Cameroonian whom I knew would refer to me as Erico.

Alphonse and Chief looked at me while Vincent was panicking and we could hear footsteps going up and down the stairs. I knew what had happened straight away.

My plan had completely backfired. I had not informed Essilor and Barthelemy that I had already been to the client's house and scammed him out of five thousand dollars because I had no plans of telling them. They had been sitting at Pechatniki hostel waiting for me, when the two weeks had elapsed without me showing up, they simply decided to go back to the client's house and activate the plan themselves, after all, I had done the groundwork and the client was interested. They were welcomed into the client's household in Sevastopolskaya and were taken hostage at gunpoint. They had been pistol-whipped and beaten for three days until Essilor told them he knew how to reach me. He was taken back to the hostel where he persuaded Francis to give him my telephone number in Babushkinskaya.

Now Barthelemy and Essilor where downstairs and Essilor was the one calling me Erico. I still did not confide to Alphonse and Chief what I had done and what was going on, instead Alphonse went into the kitchen, lit the cooker and started burning evidence of fake dollars. While the doorbell rang, the door was being banged even louder, 'Erico! Erico! Erico!' my name was being called from outside.

Alphonse considered jumping from the third-floor window into the garden, which would have been possible in the winter. Saul and I accomplished such a feat in Stavropol during the raid at the hostel but that was during the peak of winter, when the snow was about five feet deep; jumping from this window would have resulted in severe injury.

Chief just sat down and pondered. In the soles of his shoes he had money to the amount of around six million roubles. There was no cocaine in the house and the clients had never met him or Vincent. Though Chief and Vincent were panicking, there was hope for them. I insisted we call the police but Chief refused saying, 'If the police come to your house you are marked.' This was it for Alphonse and I, for me especially: not only had I duped the clients, I had placed Barthelemy and Essilor at death's door. They were now being held hostage, not to be released until Alphonse and I were in custody.

Sleep left our eyes that night, Chief and Alphonse asked all sorts of questions, I just went with the simple fact that we had been caught and that was it. In the early hours of the morning, Vincent and Chief decide to brave it and go downstairs, they had nothing to hide but still they panicked. Alphonse and I looked through the bedroom window. As soon as Chief and Vincent came into view, a man got out of a blue Volga, grabbed Vincent by the hand, and gave him a couple of slaps in the face. Vincent gave out a big shout, 'I die today.' Chief suffered the same fate.

Chief spoke a bit of Russian but Vincent was far more fluent; they insisted there was no one else in the house, but this all fell on deaf ears as the clients were determined to check the house for themselves. I was calculating the distance between the window and the ground, the idea of jumping played on my mind. As if it would help, I went into the room and hid myself under the bed. Alphonse had found a small cupboard in the living room and compressed himself inside.

When the clients got into the house, the first place they looked was where Alphonse was hiding. I heard Alphonse screaming as he was being punched, then they booted the door to the room I was hiding in and lifted the bed up, shouting, 'Here he is!' I was then dragged from underneath the bed kicking and screaming. I was punched and kicked nonstop for I don't know how long. I was hit with the kitchen stool on my back until it broke; they used everything they could lay their hands on and battered us. I remember some yoghurt falling onto the shoes of one of the clients, he insisted I licked it clean; I did so with no hesitation. We were beaten, battered.

'Where is our money?' We were called all the names under the sun. I recognised the two clients but they had brought two other guys, who were Russians. One of them was wearing a military uniform and was standing by the wall next to the door: he remained silent and had the cold eyes of a killer.

I had given up. This was it for me.

I looked at Alphonse, who was bleeding—head and legs swollen, for they were using the legs of the stools to hit us without mercy. This beating was only punctuated by questions of, 'Where is our money?' I was punched so hard I fell into the bathroom and landed next to some imperial leather soap. As I fell, I remembered how my friend, Mephistopheles, used to convince his mum that he was not well and unable to go to school by biting into a bar of soap; he would pretend to faint and the soap would form unwanted mucous in his mouth, that he spewed out.

When I hit the ground, I reached for the soap and took a bite, and using my tongue I generated enough fluid to turn it into unwanted mucous. I was dragged back into the room and the punches flowed; when I fell back down, I started foaming in the mouth. I was shaking. Growing up in the village, we had a friend called Liombe, who had died from a fainting fit. I had seen Liombe fainting a couple of times and I mimicked his body movements.

The client kicked me in my ribs but I did not cry out in pain or anything, I just jerked and shook as if I was at death's door. I heard Vincent saying I was faking it. Of course I was faking it. What else was I left with? The more they kicked, the more I ignored the pain, I just carried on spitting mucous, until the Russian guys asked my attackers to stop.

'The black is dying,' he said. The guy stopped and slapped me on my face. Knowing that my trick was working I started taking

119

long punctuated breaths, exactly as my maternal grandmother did before she died. I was shaking my legs like a chicken whose throat had been cut, I shook my hands and jerked my body. The Russian guy then said, 'Come on, let's take them to the cars.' I was still shaking and jerking and pretended I couldn't walk. I was wearing trainers, a black pair of jeans, a white sleeveless top that was now blood-stained and an unzipped Adidas jacket.

One of the clients helped Alphonse and he limped slowly in front of me. I walked as slow as possible, avoiding any eye contact in case my eyes betrayed my plans. When we got to the bottom of the stairs and outside the house, Alphonse was taken to a Volga that was located to the right of the building. This was my cue. The guy who was holding me had his hands on my jacket but not on me, he had assumed I was too frail to attempt any sudden moves but he was wrong. Alphonse knew what I was going to do and said, 'Eric, don't do it.'

My need for flight overtook all reasoning within me. Pretending to fall, I unzipped my jacket completely, stretching my whole body forwards and my arms backwards. The jacket came off and was left in the guy's hands. I was free momentarily as I turned and started running towards the left of the building. The driver, who was sitting in his Lada, opened the driver's door but I instinctively folded my fists and my hands went through the window, smashing the glass and forcing the door back towards the driver. I was derailed briefly but I kept running.

I could hear the Russian guy shouting to the onlookers who had stopped, 'Stop him. Stop him. He's a thief.' I retorted to the onlookers, 'I'm not a thief, those guys are drug dealers, call the police.' In the confusion that followed, the onlookers stood dumbfounded, were they to stop a poor black man who was being chased by drug dealers or help their Russian compatriots stop a thief? I ran towards the main road, traffic was not that bad given that it was a motorway and I ran across with complete disregard to running into cars. I looked behind me and instead of crossing the road, the guys were running towards the Babushkinskaya metro, as if they had read my mind.

The traffic police officers that were sitting on the other side of the road did not move, they must have noticed me. I ran as fast as I could, I ran down the stairs and onto Babushkinskaya station. The conductor, an old lady, frowned in despair as to what could have possibly happened to me and we faced each other briefly. I had no ticket and said to the conductor, in Russian, that there had been a diplomatic scandal and that I had to go report the incident to the Cameroonian Embassy and that I was being followed by a gang of criminals. I would not see my reflection until I got to Sheremetyevo airport. She looked at me cynically but opened the barriers, just in time too as I could see the guys coming down the stairs. I scrambled on a train to Sheremetyevo airport and sat down; everyone else moved, probably thinking I had been the victim of some vicious skinhead attack.

The checking-in had already started by the time I reached the airport and Vincent was there with my Zimbabwean passport. He was in the company of another guy who he said was going to help me through the immigration controls and checks. I had given Vincent a hundred dollars for this service.

At the checkout desk was a young and very beautiful Russian woman; her mouth almost fell off her face when she saw me. She enquired if I had been in an accident then motioned to her colleague and whispered something into his ears; he disappeared and a few seconds later brought some towels and handed them to me. I was then ushered to the airport toilets to clean myself up. My head was covered in little golf ball-sized bumps, my face was blood stained, my jaw swollen on both sides, the taste of soap had seized control of my taste buds, dried blood was all over my T-shirt, all over my jeans, all over my shoes while my arms and legs were swollen. That was when the pain hit me. The adrenaline had taken me to the airport but once I saw my reflection in the mirror, the gravity of the situation hit home—there were Russian men in

Moscow actively looking for me. I thought of the fate that awaited Alphonse and was so glad I was finally leaving Russia.

I cleaned my face and I tried pushing down some of the little mountains on my head. I did the best job I could. When I got back to the checkout desk a flight attendant, who had been called, insisted that there was no way I would be allowed to get onto the flight, that I was unfit and too sick to travel.

'Jejayeeeeeeeee!' is how my ancestors would shout if you find yourself in a terrible and impossible situation. I cried, I begged, I pleaded but to no avail. I told them only death awaited me if I should be returned to the streets of Moscow. The flight attendant refused and walked away, insisting I needed proper medical attention and they were not prepared to let me onto the aeroplane, thereby putting other passengers at risk. Vincent and his friend had vamoosed. The Russian girl handed back my passport and closed the gates. My fate was sealed. For the first time in my life I contemplated suicide.

Chapter 13

Not only was I lost, not only was I stranded, not only was the fact that I didn't even have a tree whose leaves could be a canopy for the night, I was paranoid and sceptical of everyone with tanned skin and dark hair. Most of all, the worms in my stomach where forming a chorus, they were shouting, 'We want food. We want food.'

I had so much anger burgeoning inside of me it had increased my wrinkles. When I sat down on the train everyone else gave me a wide berth. I was waiting for just one skinhead to even gesture in my direction and there was going to be murder. I hated my father's family even more. I was planning all kinds of evil that I would unleash on them. I couldn't think, my stomach was eating itself slowly, the train was even slower and it took an age before getting into Belorusskaya. From there I took the brown line three stops down to Kiyevskaya.

I exited the train station, crossed the road and went past McDonald's. My hunger got worse. I carried on walking, past the offices and stopped just before the road veers left towards the diplomatic corpus, then I walked straight into an attaché of the British Embassy. There was a girl at the reception and other workers at the back who were all visible. I remember her name: Sophie. She asked how she could be of help. I narrated to her the incident of the previous night and how I had managed to escape. I told her I was the victim of a drug deal that went wrong, I was hoping now that I was a Zimbabwean and that I could persuade my former colonial masters to come to my aid. She took notes, not believing what she was hearing. I knew Prime Minister Tony Blair and President Mugabe of Zimbabwe were still friends at this time, and I was hoping this entente cordiale would work in my favour and the British Embassy could hide me or help me leave the country. I was desperate and did whatever came to mind. I told Sophie I was extremely hungry; that was the first time I ever ate tiny sausages in beans and tomato sauce with one potato here another potato there. She wrote everything down but, in the end, said that while she would create a file for me, as far as she was concerned, I had to escalate the matter with my own embassy, the Zimbabwean embassy. Yeah right.

Alphonse had introduced me to a black American who worked at the American Embassy. When I knocked on his door, his wife opened and said he was still at work but she allowed me to wait for him to come home. She offered me sandwiches and hot chocolate, and I munched on them as if there was no tomorrow. When the husband arrived home, I told him the same story I had told Sophie earlier in the day. The truth is I knew all this was futile, I knew that I would only be referred to the Zimbabwean Embassy. I just wanted a place to rest, to sleep, to contemplate—at least for one night. He wrote down everything I said and at around 8 p.m. apologised and said I must leave his house.

As I walked back towards Kiyevskaya underground station, I thought about ending my life. Who would know? Who would care? As I got closer to the station, the thought of suicide increased, it was as if the gods had decided my fate. I had heard of people committing suicide by jumping in front of a train. Most of the newspaper reports said that these people where intoxicated by homemade vodka. In fact, many years later, while I worked as head of security in HMV in Croydon, a very good friend of mine who worked for Virgin Media, Richard Asamoah (RIP), committed suicide by jumping on the fast train tracks in Streatham, south east London. If I was going to be successful in this mission, I needed a fast train, not one that slowed down as it approached the station. I wanted suicide—not a broken bone or an injury that meant I was fluctuating between death and consciousness.

I stood on the Kiyevskaya station platform and waited. I had made up my mind, I had given up, I had reached the bottom of Dante's Peak—this was it for me. My body was with me but my spirit was gone. I felt that gnashing of teeth; death was whispering to me, daring me to jump. I had lost all that made me human, I was a ghost, I was floating, I was flying. I could see my adopted sister Monjowa, as I remember her, her beautiful smile, her bubbly personality. Sister Monjowa had a charming personality. I was in pain for Sister Monjowa who was placed under pressure by my father's family to reject me that day at the Paul's chambers. I knew she loved me. As I stood on the platform about to end my life, how I wished she could hug me and tell me all will be fine. I could feel my tears sinking inside of me. I was a man: we don't cry.

As the train approached the station, I could see my mother's face. She had more wrinkles than usual, she looked sad and she was saying something but the noise meant I couldn't hear her. All I could hear was the loudspeaker on the platform saying, 'This train will not be stopping at this station.' It was now or never, my time had come: this was the day the gods had written, today my name was to be erased from the book of life forever, today I was ending my little sojourn here on earth. If in life I didn't have the chance to question my father, I was ready to join him in the land of the spirits and ask him to right the wrongs his family had brought onto the shoulders of my mother and I.

As the train approached I could hear the tracks squeaking, then I heard my mother's voice again. She was shouting my name, 'Ngalle! Ngalle!' I smiled, for this is the name my mother calls me when I have done something good. She said, 'If you kill yourself, I will wake you up and beat you until you die again.' That's my mother for you: Iya Sarah Efeti Kange.

*

I remember one afternoon my mother was tired from work – I nagged and nagged her for food, she lost her temper and hit me with her workbag. She had forgotten that in her bag was a large glass bottle, and the impact on my right elbow meant the bottle broke and cut deep into my flesh and blood spewed out. My mother cried, she slapped me on the back of my head saying, 'Look at what you've made me do? Your stubbornness is going to kill me one of these days.' In tears, she hailed a taxi and carried me to the hospital.

*

As the train got even closer, I remembered one of my mother's stories about a farmer's son who was warned never to sigh or show any signs of tiredness when transporting cotton from his master's farm to his master's shed. Unfortunately for him, the load was too heavy for a twelve-year-old boy and when he reached the top of the hill, he sighed and sat down on the fallen branch of a buma tree and fell asleep. In his sleep he saw the devil and his friend Jukuke, who came and took him away; his parents never saw him again. This story never made any sense to me until recently, when I asked my mother about it; she said it was a story that was told by the French to the English Cameroonians to ensure they worked nonstop at the plantations whilst the French reaped the benefits. This was my mother's understanding of French colonial Cameroon.

I could see the light at the end of the tunnel and it was that of a fast approaching train. I lifted my heels and leaned forward. I saw my uncles and aunties from my mother's side of the family, all dead now. They were waving at me to cross over to the other side. With their waves and smiles, I decided to join them. Suddenly I heard this loud shout and a tug on my shoulders, 'Young man, have you gone mad? Are you trying to kill yourself?' I looked up and the train went past at full speed. I had missed my chance; today was not the day the gods had set out for me, my name was not on the list after all. It suddenly dawned on me that I had tried committing suicide.

The voice belonged to Sasha, a young officer in charge of security at both Kiyevskaya underground and overground stations. She backed me against the marble wall and asked to see some identification. She spoke English with grace and purity. She reminded me of the officer who had stopped us at Mineralnye Vody, the buffer zone between Russia and Chechnya in southern Russia.

Sasha looked like Demi Moore in the film *Ghost*, only more beautiful. An angel had saved me. She had short, curly, dark hair that just graced the top part of her ears. Her eyes were hazel and her lashes long and thick. She smiled and spoke at the same time. She had thick full lips unlike any other Russian woman I had seen.

When she took my hand hers were so soft. The only other hands I have touched as soft are those of Edgar Davids, the Dutch footballer when he played for Tottenham (at the time I worked as a security guard for Lilywhites in Piccadilly Circus, and upon recognising Edgar we arranged amongst the security team to trigger the alarm when he left the store. He was stunned but when we told him it was a prank, he laughed and shook our hands and took pictures with us. His hands were unnaturally soft for a man).

Sasha's uniform fitted perfectly in all the right places and she looked more like a pilot than a police officer. She told me her parents had been stationed in East Berlin but she had returned to Voronezh, her parents' village, just before the collapse of the Berlin Wall. She spent two years in the police academy in Moscow, backed up by her flare for languages—she spoke French, Russian, English, German and Polish—and at the age of twenty-three, she was relocated to Moscow and stationed at Kiyevskaya station as head of security. As she said all these things, in my head I was thinking that she was a spy.

She took me to the overground section of Kiyevskaya station, where her office was based, and introduced me to her colleagues saying, 'This is Mr Thambvani from Zimbabwe.' She proceeded to tell them how she had saved me from committing suicide. They laughed in unison when one of them said, 'A black man committing suicide in the train station? Things must be really bad in Africa.'

Sasha gave me tea and bread with assorted meat, she also gave me a sleeping bag and showed me a bench inside the overground station where I could rest. The crowd didn't bother me; the haggard looks of the many different passengers, awaiting relatives, departing, arriving, their sight did not bother me. The fact that I had attempted suicide did not plague me—my mind was clean as a whistle. I was off to the land of nod. I slept soundly, and not a single dream came my way.

The following day Sasha brought me toothpaste and a toothbrush. I was in so much pain I could not move my body. My legs, hands, lips and eyes were all sore and swollen, my clothes stuck to my body. Sasha took me to a place, some sort of mission, where the homeless people in that region gathered for food.

A couple of days later I caught sight of my friend Alphonse. I had seen him from the distance and noticed he was limping along. I shadowed him to see if he was being followed. He had one of my shoes and one of his shoes on. When I finally approached, he didn't shake my hand but just looked at me with disdain and scorn. He told me he had been taken to Komsomolskaya and held at the house of the clients. He had met Essilor and Barthelemy and they had told him what had happened, how I had duped them and taken their client away from them. Alphonse went on to say I should have informed him and Chief, but there was no point crying over spilled beans. He told me the clients were actively looking for me and that I must avoid Essilor and Barthelemy as they too were vying for my blood. Alphonse was only saved by the fact that he'd been saving his money at the diplomatic corpus in Kiyevskaya. Upon his detention, the clients took him there and he handed them two thousand dollars, which was how he'd secured his release. That was the last time I saw Alphonse.

I spent around a week in Kiyevskaya overground train station, sleeping among passengers. Some came, some left and some, like me, who had nowhere to go, remained. There were many homeless people in that station. The officers who patrolled the station would wait until one was deep in the land of nod and snoring before coming to wake one up and ask, 'Have you got a ticket?' Those without tickets would be asked to leave the station but as soon as the officers left, they would return. It was a cat and mouse situation. This particular morning though, Sasha did not bring me breakfast. Her smile had disappeared. Her perfect makeup, her mannequin face, looked rough, dishevelled, and little tears dropped from her eyes as she spoke to me.

I hugged her. She sobbed loudly. She was going to Voronezh— her father had been shot and killed during a botched robbery at their family home. She hugged me even tighter, and it seemed an age before she let go; time stopped, passers-by stared. I have woken up many nights dreaming of this moment. I am rubbish at painting, otherwise I would have painted this moment, as it is forever ingrained in my mind. I was flying, floating—this was where I wanted to be, this moment.

She reached into her wallet and gave me an envelope and said, 'This is two hundred roubles. I will be back soon.' Her security friends were looking at me with disdain. She took a few steps backwards. She crossed the road and slowly disappeared into the crowd. I never saw Sasha again. Sometimes I have wondered if she was a ghost or an angel or an Ogbanje Child (children who come and go, a phenomenon common in West African society).

That was the beginning of the end of my sojourn at Kiyevskaya overground station. Sasha leaving brought with it a change of guards and the new guys were hostile, just doing their jobs I guess, and if you didn't have a ticket that was it. It was during the chaos of this cat and mouse between train security staffs and us the homeless and stateless that I got talking to another black guy. I cannot remember his name but he was an Ibo Nigerian, and two

Russians joined and entertained us with vodka concealed in a Coca-Cola bottle. Again, I was the translator as the Ibo boy didn't speak the language. During the conversation, the two Russians said, 'We have a house not far away from here and you can come and stay overnight.' This was the best news ever, the Ibo was happy, I was happy, they took us to the platform and we jumped on the train. As we sat on the train we laughed and joked. I thought nothing of it; this is how stupid and naïve I was.

After a while an announcement was made by the train driver, 'This train is now heading for the depot.' All the carriages were empty, we were the last people on the train, which was in total darkness. Yes, we were the last people to get off the train, we followed the tracks, and the smaller of the Russians had a torch. There were no houses to be seen. Once our eyes had adjusted to the darkness, the only thing we could see was the train tracks.

The Ibo guy turns to me and says in pidgin, 'Let's run, these guys are thieves.' I didn't have to wait for a second invite and we started running down the tracks. The Russian guys were shouting, 'Stop. Stop. We're going to fuck you, we're going to fuck your mothers to hell.' In the distance we could see a light and we ran towards it—it was the depot. When we got there, the night workers must have thought we were devils, two black men in the middle of nowhere out of breath. Some were washing the trains whilst other sat playing cards and drinking vodka.

They walked towards us with folded fists. I told them that we were being followed by two Russians who had attempted to rob us. Stupidly, or maybe they didn't anticipate anyone to be at the depot, the two Russians came in and were still mouthing off. That was the worst mistake they made that night: they were battered by the guys on duty and dragged out of the depot. We spent the night with those guys at the depot until the morning shift took over. We were not asked for tickets and the train took us back to Kiyevskaya. I had had enough. I sold my sleeping bag to the Ibo boy for fifteen roubles and decided to go to Pechatniki. If I was going to be killed in Russia, I figured it would be better if I were among my own people.

The skies were extra dark that evening in Moscow, and as dreadful as it was, Pechatniki was my only destination. The prospect of meeting Essilor and Barthelemy pained me, knowing fully well what I had done: I had placed them in harm's way. According to what Alphonse had told me, even though Essilor and Barthelemy claimed to the clients that they didn't know my intentions, the fact that they were associated with me meant they had received some beatings. I stayed on the train as it went around and around central Moscow. As I drifted into the land of nod, I could see my mother.

*

I had brought a girl back to the house and my mother was asleep in her room. I only discovered this not to be true when my mother kicked the door open. Both the girl and I were standing in front of my mother naked. I quickly put on some shorts and my mother used one of my cravats to tie our hands together and started marching us down the street, past my father's compound and halfway to the top of the hill. We met my brother and his friend Charleston Ellison (they had been out drinking) and my mother explained to them what she'd caught me doing.

She said she was taking us to her parents. My brother and Charleston Ellison pleaded with my mother not to be so harsh. As they begged, she was crying, and I was thinking of my street credibility. All their pleas were falling on deaf ears; my mother had her mind made up. This was the case until my brother said he was going to see his friend who had a small shop just up the road, and would buy my mother three bottles of Amstel Beer. My mother finally climbed down but warned me vehemently, 'Have you grown horns? Are you the child of the devil? If you want to start fucking, go and find your own house, do not bring the devil under my roof.'

After that night I was forever indebted to Charleston Ellison and my big brother. This marked a thaw in the hostile relationship I had with my brother: he did love me really. My mother and I laugh about this incident whenever we talk on the phone. As for the girl, she never spoke to me again. I am sure she had told her friends about the incident because every time I went past her house into Longstreet, to buy puff and beans, she would burst into laughter among her friends.

*

I changed trains at Kurskaya and joined the green line, and I carried on until I reached Pechatniki, not knowing that coming to Pechatniki would be the worse decision I ever made. It was here I came closest to being killed; not by Russian skinheads, but by fellow English Cameroonians. My own kind, my own people.

Chapter 14

All the rough, red-eyed and long throated black people I had first seen at Sheremetyevo airport in May in 1997 were here in Pechatniki. I met Miranda (remember this name) who pestered me for money along the corridors of Pechatniki, I met Ndumbe (who went on to date Miranda) who told me old wives' tales about knowing my friends back home, I met Sister Hanna whose family hail from New Layout in Tiko, I met Ifeoma the Great, I met Derek (a taxi driver who dated one of my nieces), I met Weston (who was accused of picking out people at the airport he'd take to his shack and, after relieving them of their money, would leave them at the mercy of skinheads) and most of all I met Jerome who became spiritually connected to me as soon as we met.

Of all the seventy or so Cameroonians who resided at Pechatniki, only around ten were registered students, the rest were victims of human trafficking. Having suffered my fate, they too were stranded in a state of limbo. The Cameroon Embassy did not have money to repatriate them. Most started selling cocaine, sexual promiscuity was rife and ill treatment and barbarity dished out. People did whatever they could to gain floor space for sleeping, all kinds of alliances were formed. I slept in Ndumbe's room and on any given night there would be at least fourteen people in the room. Francis would be having sex with Mandy, Ndumbe with Miranda, while the rest of us would be wanking or permanently sleepless. The only person who didn't have sex was a guy called Touré, who begged and pleaded for Sister Hanna to sleep with him but Sister Hanna was a lady of class and standards. Life in Pechatniki had a routine. By six in the morning everyone left the hostel, some people had found work loading and offloading trucks in Rigskayaya market, while one guy, Peter, ran a small market stall. Peter was well posh and his room well-maintained. Those who didn't work left the hostel during the day for fear of police raids.

The girls had it worst. They had to cling to boys to make ends meet, hence sexual gambling and promiscuity was the norm.

Those who had jobs (I am using the term loosely as there were no contracts or laws to protect them) always came back with stories of being stopped by the police or skinheads.

Pechatniki was across the road from a skinhead headquarters. People preferred to walk in groups rather than catch the bus as that meant one had to go past the skinhead headquarters; these guys where not shy and attacked in broad daylight with no remorse. I remember I made the mistake once of catching the train alone on a Sunday. In my compartment there was just a babushka and myself. Next to the door was a group of clean-shaven boys, girls and men wearing long boots, their jeans with chains that dangled all the way to their boots. They carried blades and knuckle dusters. They looked at me piercingly and were gesturing with their hands, telling me they were going to slit my throat. They were aged between twelve and forty years old, one of them had a tattoo of a cross on his forehead, his ears and on his nose; they all had little crosses on them. They sipped from a green bottle that they passed around.

When the train came to a stop the babushka asked me in Russian, 'Young man, could you please help me with my bag of potatoes?' I picked up the bag and held her hand, helping her off the train. The group of skinheads moved toward the door, held it open for a few seconds before letting it close, they never came out. I took deep breaths while they gave me all sorts of gestures from middle fingers to flashing me their buttocks. The babushka then said to me, 'Please go home. Today is your lucky day.'

Once again, my understanding of the Russian language had saved me from a severe beating and God knows what else. By helping the babushka, I had effectively saved my life; given how respectfully old people are treated, the skinheads had seen my gesture as friendly even though it pained them a great deal. When I got back to the hostel and told this story, Ifeoma the Great said that the skinheads, apparently, had a member of parliament in the Russian Duma, who had declared Sunday a day of bashing all dark-skinned people.

All in all, things were good. I had met with Barthelemy and Essilor and had bought them pepper soup, we drank plenty of beer. Essilor forgave me and although our friendship never got back to where it once had been, we developed a mutual respect. Barthelemy on the other hand never forgave me and, when the time came, he exercised his revenge on me.

Ndumbe had been pestering me about helping him obtain his registration at the university and would invite me to share breakfast with him and Miranda. He had four hundred dollars but the fees were a thousand dollars. After a lot of persuasion I decided to go with him to his university, which was how I met the rector of Moscow State University who was in charge of international students, and effectively laid down the foundations to becoming a human trafficker. I had gone full circle: from meeting human trafficking foot soldiers in Cameroon, to meeting the barons at Sheremetyevo and now meeting the source of all those university invitation letters. He was a tall skinny dude, had no idea that the invitation letters he had been issuing to Diamonds and his entourage, who were spread across Moscow, were responsible for human trafficking on such an unimaginable scale.

He greeted us and offered a cup of tea as was customary. 'So, how can I help you?' he asked quietly after we were done with the pleasantries. This was my moment. I told him that I was Ndumbe's guardian, that I had finished my studies at Stavropol State University and was on my way back to Cameroon. I told him I had asked for some money from back home to pay Ndumbe's fees and that I was going to pay two hundred dollars, with the rest in a month's time. He hesitated at first but then agreed. I excused myself and took Ndumbe outside where he handed me the four hundred dollars, he also handed me his passport. I asked Ndumbe to wait for me outside, placed two hundred dollars in the passport as promised and handed it over to the rector and kept two hundred for myself. The rector removed the two hundred dollars, placed it in his pocket and called for his secretary. He handed over Ndumbe's passport to her and muttered something about registration.

We were then told to wait at the receptionist in the corridor. After an hour or so we were called back, the secretary handed Ndumbe his passport with a six-month's student registration visa inside. Ndumbe was none the wiser; I didn't tell him a single thing. This was the second seed I planted that would become cause for the attempted murder that was to take place a couple of weeks later.

Before leaving the campus, I went to see the rector again and told him I had another friend who wanted an exit visa so he could travel to Zimbabwe. He advised me to come back and see him the next day. When I returned, he took me into a police barracks. Everyone there greeted him with warmth, and two young officers searched us. I was then introduced to the head of Russia's third immigration district. Once the introductions were done, the rector left. I explained my problem—I wanted to return to my country, Zimbabwe, but I needed an exit visa. I handed my passport over and he sent me to another office, where two female secretaries photocopied my passport and gave me a letter and told me to take it to the post office. I handed my passport across the counter along with the letter. The lady looked at it for a few minutes before issuing me with some forms. Once I had finished, I handed them over, along with my passport and seventy-five roubles. She gave me another letter to take to the immigration office inside the police barracks and I was searched once more before being shown upstairs.

I handed my passport to the secretary with the letter from the post office and was told to wait. Another hour passed before my name was called, 'Mr Ocimile Thambvani?' I had completely forgotten what my new name was. When I went to the cubicle, I was handed my passport with three months' Moscow residential status and an exit visa. Maybe, just maybe, my ancestors had not abandoned me after all. I was now officially a Zimbabwean citizen with residency and an exit visa, all I had to do now was to look for money to get an air ticket to Zimbabwe from where I would hitchhike back to Cameroon. As I left the hostel I remembered when I was ten years old.

*

We had been warned not to play with the nest of a weaverbird. There was a eucalyptus tree bang in the middle of the compound that hosted a community of weaverbirds but one day while trying to get to Mola Mongambe's farm and harvest some pineapples, I came across a nest. It had three weaverbird chicks inside and ignoring the warnings of our elders, I took the nest with the little chicks to the house and played with them and fed them.

By the time my mother got home I had been struck by an intense fever and had fainted. When I woke up, Aunty Frida our neighbour was in our house, helping my mother with me. I was burning up. Cold towels were placed on my head and Aunty Frida placed a spoon between my teeth to prevent me from biting my tongue. Even though I was at death's door my mother still slapped me from time to time saying, 'Have you gone nuts? Why did you bring the weaverbird's nest into the house?'

The following day, my mother took me to visit a juju man in WoPa Takesh called Mola Mwambo to perform a ritual on me. My mother brought with her a cockerel as payment for his services and a little chick. Using his hands, Mola Mwambo ripped the chick's head right off and made a circular motion round his head with the chick's head. The poor chick was still alive, flapping, as he handed me the decapitated head and told me to do the same circular motion around my head. He then took me to the backyard of his house and I had to do the same circular motion with the chick's head again. I chucked the chick's head over my shoulder and walked into the house without looking back. In the kitchen the rest of the chick was placed in charcoal, along with dried matove and palm nut chaffs. I basked in the smoke until the chick disappeared. Mola Mwambo then told me to go home, that I was cured. Lo and behold, I was cured and I have never suffered fainting fits again. I have often wondered what was wrong with my mother? Why didn't she just take me to the hospital?

*

I was starting to believe that all the juju things that had been blended into my body were starting to work. Here I was in the middle of Moscow, in the premises of Ivan Ivanovic Locev and had obtained a Moscow residency and an exit visa in a passport that wasn't mine. This is juju stuff. When I returned to the hostel that evening, I showed everyone my newly found status but no one knew how I had managed to obtain it. This proved to be the wrong move; I was stepping on people's toes. When the night of my kidnap and torture came, I found out the depths of displeasure I had caused amongst my own kind.

With my newfound status as a legal Zimbabwean, I had all kinds of chameleons for friends. I was thought of as the new kingpin and people came to me with all sorts of problems. I helped as much as I could. I had confided in Jerome that I had kept two hundred dollars of Ndumbe's fees and he was worried about the prospect of me going to Zimbabwe, against all his wishes. When Jerome's sister sent him three hundred dollars from Switzerland, he lent me two hundred and fifty dollars so I could buy my air ticket. The night before my second attempt at leaving Russia, Jonson and I drank at the French woman's room. We ate plenty of fufu and cow's leg—no one knew our plans.

The next morning, Jerome accompanied me to Sheremetyevo. I had a bad feeling about this second attempt at leaving Russia.

Jerome waved as I went past the first customs checkpoint, then the officials for KLM said I could not travel. They told me that I needed a transit visa for Germany and the way they looked at the passport I suspected they had realised that it wasn't me. I didn't stop long to plead with them; the worst thing that could have happened to me now was to lose my newfound Zimbabwean status. My second attempt at leaving Russia had failed. Jerome and I returned to the hostel in Pechatniki.

The only person I human trafficked was a guy called Swappo. I have heard plenty of rumours but there was only one person and one person alone, and that was Swappo. Since arriving in Russia, Swappo had lived illegally and when he heard I had a Zimbabwean passport, with an exit visa in it, he offered me one thousand dollars to buy the passport, for he too was desperate to leave Russia. I never sold my passport, instead Swappo borrowed money from Aubin and then I went with him through the routine of going to see Ivan and eventually Swappo was granted temporary residency with an exit visa in his Cameroonian passport. However, his passport was held at the immigration office until he bought his air ticket. When he returned, with a Bakossi boy called Lanna, at the time, Swappo was detained and kept in a cell for three days. However, Lanna had returned and told the people at the hostel that I had swallowed Swappo's money and that Swappo had been locked up waiting repatriation to Cameroon.

This tale amplified people's hatred for me at the hostel. A couple of days later, when I returned, I was told what had happened. I visited Swappo at the detention centre and I spoke to the guards and discovered Swappo had only been detained because he couldn't speak the language and because of his exit visa; he had was what they call in Russian a Srochnie Visa which means one had to exit the country as soon as possible, as if one had committed a crime. The next day we met Swappo at Sheremetyevo airport and immigration officers accompanied him. He boarded the aeroplane.

That was the only person whose human trafficking I initiated. When people heard the success story of Swappo, they swarmed towards me. I could have explored the situation but human trafficking was not my cup of tea.

Pechatniki itself was getting worse. There was fighting every day, drunkenness was the norm, there was no loyalty, it was a rat race, it was chaos, people had grown horns and they looked like devils, they were cursed. Pechatniki was the closest I got to experiencing hell and the gnashing of teeth—people had given up hope—people could kill and intercourse took place between frogs and princesses and vice versa just for sleeping spaces.

Three incidents occurred that put me on a good pedestal with some of the occupants of the hostel. You see, the only way of entering the hostel for those who lived there illegally, which was ninety per cent, was through the side of the hostel. You had to navigate your way through the windows on the balcony until you reached the third floor. This was less hazardous in the summer; in the winter the health and safety risks were just too great but it was during one of such winter night that one Cameroonian from Bamenda, his name was Tata McDonald, had slipped and fallen from the third floor. He had fractured his spine and lay under the snow for God knows how long.

He was only spotted when one of the security guards downstairs was doing his hourly patrol. He was half covered in snow. The guard rushed upstairs and summoned us. They had called an ambulance but needed someone to accompany Tata to the hospital. Everyone declined but I volunteered. I jumped in the ambulance with Tata and we drove to Dynamo where he was taken into emergency theatre. I thought Tata had died because he wasn't moving. They cut off his trousers with a pair of scissors and used a large syringe to prick his limbs but there was no movement and I remember my brother during one of his history classes saying that in some societies, black people were used for medical experimentation. I prayed for Tata. He eventually recovered but

140

remained in a wheelchair. His family sent money and he was eventually returned to Cameroon.

Tata was not the only one to get hurt.

Rose was very beautiful and petite. She had light brown and very smooth skin; just looking at her one could tell she had an element of class. But Pechatniki and Moscow were taking their toll on her. Pechatniki was inhumane to both sexes—there was no discrimination. On her return from work one evening, Rose had made the mistake of coming home alone instead of waiting for her friends as was customary. She got off the bus just outside the council estate that housed the skinheads and she never made it to the hostel—instead she was attacked and badly beaten. To finish her off, they had smashed a bottle on her head. The skinheads only stopped when the security guards, who were on their way to changing shifts at the hostel, heard the kerfuffle and intervened. They carried Rose into the reception at the hostel before calling an ambulance and coming up to inform us. Once again, my linguistic skill was summoned—the legal Zimbabwean was to follow the ambulance with Rose to the hospital. She was rushed into surgery, and I stayed with Rose until the following morning. I visited her in hospital a couple of times. If ever there was a black girl I would have dated whilst in Moscow, it would have been Rose. She became my forever friend and when I was being tortured at the hostel, she cried and pleaded on my behalf.

Then there was Remy.

We had nicknamed him Remy Money, because he had a laissez faire attitude towards his money. For him money came and went. In this regard, people congregated towards him, waiting until he'd had a few drinks then he would proceed to buy everyone a drink until his money was finished. He would ask those fake friends for money for a train ticket the next day but no one would give him anything. Remy was one of the strongest people I knew. Remy and I ended up working in the same shop at Rigskayaya market a couple of months later.

The routine at the hostel was like this: every Friday from six thirty onwards Eddie Grant's 'Give me Hope Joanna' would be blasted out of a ghetto blaster and people would drink and dance and then there would be fights along the corridors, sex in the lift, all sorts of debauchery, which would be followed by one of Eddie Grant's hits: 'I don't wanna dance, dance with my baby no more'. People would drink themselves into an uncontrollable stupor.

It was during one such night that, after consuming so much alcohol, Remy Money thought he had developed wings and was able to fly. He had completely forgotten that the there was a glass door separating the third-floor balcony from the landing but he ran at full speed, leaning forward, and smashed his head straight into the glass and landed on the balcony. We heard the noise and everyone came outside, there was panic as the glass had sliced Remy's face from his jaw to the top of his skull; he was lying there, bleeding. I rushed downstairs and asked the guards to telephone an ambulance. Once again, I accompanied someone to the hospital.

Chapter 15

Jerome had finally gotten in touch with his sister in Switzerland and she had sent him two hundred dollars so that day after work at the market we went to Akhotny Ryad. We visited the Kremlin and even had a roast chicken, Armenian style, with soft white bread and two bottles of Coca-Cola. It so transpired that Jerome's uncle was the late Pa Takesh. I knew Pa Takesh had died under mysterious circumstances according to village news so it was mysterious that even Jerome was apprehensive about attending the funeral. Jerome has promised to give me compensation for the killing of Evenya'a' Mboli, my goat, by his uncle.

Jerome grew up in the village of Bokwango. His father was a palapala (traditional wrestling) referee and Mola Pa Takesh was a wrestler, as was Jerome. I have asked Jerome if he was the molikilikili that had brought me down during that wrestling match in Wonganga village but he denies it. Maybe Mola Pa Takesh had planned it all along—he had known how good Jerome was and had given Jerome a bit of village concoction and that is how I was brought down. Maybe Jerome was made to swear an oath of confidentiality but he insists it wasn't him.

Jerome was indeed worried about attending the funeral of late Mola Pa Takesh. It was rumoured that his uncle had evolved from simply dancing with nganya (a village juju that only came out at night) into a little juju man who used his magic potions do all sorts of things. It was even said he used his juju to make the wife of Mola Monoko fall madly in love with him (all rumours I must insist).

Jerome never calls me Eric Ngalle, instead he had ordained and given me two names: Yomadene (something big) and Epassamoto (half stone half human), both gods, custodians of the Bakweri

143

tradition and people. On a bright day, if you pour a good amount of palm wine on the ground and called upon the name of Epassamoto you could see him waving at you from one of the many hills that formed Mount Fako. As for Yomadene, the last we heard Ekulekule, a tortoise, tied him to a tree. The tortoise in the Bakweri mythology is very clever. Yomadene was insisting on marrying the daughter of Ekulekule, however Ekulekule was not happy about the situation. He said he would give Yomadene his blessing on condition that Yomadene visits a dentist because according to Ekulekule, Yomadene's breath stinks for he had yellow teeth and brown gums.

Yomadene did not know what dentists did in their surgeries but Ekulekule was happy to demonstrate. Using ropes from the bamboo plant, Ekulekule tied Yomadene to an iroko tree and using barbwire, he made a chain across Yomadene's teeth. In fact it is rumoured that in the Bakweri mythology, Yomadene was the first black god to wear braces.

Late at night, if you look towards the back end of Wonya Morake in Buea town towards the direction of Weli and listen carefully, you can hear Yomadene shouting. You can even see his shadow moving, and most of all you can see the reflection of his teeth at night. According to the latest report from the elders, Yomadene has issued a fatwa on the head of Ekulekule.

Even now when Jerome and I talk, our conversation is spent with us doing the traditional dance over the telephone and Jerome calling me either Yomadene or Epassamoto.

As we crossed the road towards Pechatniki hostel, Jerome and I were playing a traditional game called Izruki, Immukka (we have arrived, we have not arrived) where he will place his hands behind my shoulders and whatever he said, I would say the opposite. This was our childhood reminiscence. All the village children played this game in order to minimise the distance between school and home and ignore the hunger that made our stomachs sing in iambic pentameter. When we got to the hostel Jerome said,

'Immukka, we have arrived.' Jerome and I were birds of the same feather. The hostel was eerily quiet, there was only one guard at the reception, and as we waved he didn't even look up from his newspaper. We quickly climbed the stairs towards the third floor; there was no one in the corridors, no music was playing, which was bizarre because around this time everyone would have been back from their daily routines of running from the police or working at the market and people would be popping from room to room.

Jerome went towards another room while I knocked on Ndumbe's door. Patrick opened the door but he held his head down and there was no eye contact and once again this was strange because Patrick would normally greet me and share some bread and talk about all the verbal racism he suffered at the bakery. But not today. As I entered the room it was like a court chambers, people were seated in circular format and there was a space in the middle with a stool. The curtain was drawn, Ndumbe was talking with Miranda, Barthelemy, The Bull and Ngobese, who, as it transpired, were the judge, jury and executioner.

Without any warning, The Bull ran from the back of the room and head-butted me point blank in the face. As I fell to the floor there was a stampede followed by a flurry of kicks to my ribs, my buttocks and my neck. I lay in a foetal position protecting my face but Ngobese and The Bull hauled me back up and dragged me into the bathroom. The Bull, who had been nominated the ringleader, demanded I take off all my clothes. When I refused, I was stripped right down to my boxer shorts. Then I heard Ndumbe shouting, 'Eric! Where is my money?' That was when I realised what had happened.

Earlier in the day, the rector had come to the hostel looking for me: the four weeks had expired and I had not been to pay the rest of Ndumbe's fees. During this routine visit he had asked for me in Ndumbe's room. While there, he had told Ndumbe that he owed eight hundred dollars instead of the six hundred as Ndumbe thought. Ngobese and The Bull insisted on stripping me naked. I said they would have to kill me first, at which point Miranda and Lanna both shouted, 'Just kill the bastard.'

I don't even know why Lanna was getting involved. At first, I thought maybe it was a tribal thing—all but two people who placed their hands on me on that day were Bakossi.

Around two months earlier in Minsk, a Cameroonian called Ngwa Movawo had been beaten and as life was slipping away from him, his haggard body was carried and abandoned outside the police station in the snow. His beating was reported to the police as a racist attack, but evidence later collected indicated that Cameroonians perpetrated the gruesome crime. He had been stripped naked, his penis electrocuted and he had been burnt with knives and kicked to death.

He had been accused of stealing money belonging to another Cameroonian. To add more grievance to his family, a few weeks after he had been killed, he was found to be innocent. I, on the other hand, was guilty. I had taken two hundred dollars of Ndumbe's four hundred dollars, I had attempted to leave Russia for the second time, I had duped Essilor and Barthelemy's client, I had not bought The Bull and Ngobese enough drinks, I had not lent any money to Miranda, the vultures were circling. The fate of the late Ngwa Movawo was to befall me. The scene was perfect, it was just a matter of re-enactment, and tonight was the night. I was placed on the stool in the middle of the room and people took turns punching me. The noise brought in Ifeoma the Great, who was in tears. Jerome was also crying. Aubin pleaded on my behalf but it fell on deaf ears, there was no way they could intervene. My worst fear occurred when Lanna went and bought a crate of Baltika 9. I knew the alcohol would only make matters worse and it did.

The Bull and Ngobese brought out two knives and placed them on top of the cooker and waited. Lanna smashed his bottle of Baltika 9 and rushed forward towards me but he was held and pinned back by Jerome. Abraham had blood-red eyes. Rose could not bear looking at me; she dreaded my fate.

Every time The Bull or Barthelemy landed a blow, the whole room cheered. This is how mad Pechatniki got: the people who were punching and beating me up were only doing so because they would be guaranteed sexual favours, small meals and a sleeping space.

Then the torture began.

Once the knives were red hot from the cooker The Bull and Barthelemy took it in turns placing the knives on my body. They started with the back of my neck. You know the noise that comes when fish or meat is placed into a heated frying pan? Well that was the noise from the back of my neck. I didn't move just in case The Bull was tempted to start cutting my neck. Once the knife began getting cold it was returned to the cooker and the next hot knife used. All in all I was burnt on my neck, my back, my knees and my ankles. The Bull even stabbed me on my right knee. The whole room smelled of burning flesh; the smell of burnt human flesh is not that different from goat meat or roasted pig.

As the alcohol flowed the torture continued. They would say, 'Just kill him and get it over with.' Lanna and Miranda were the leaders in this chorus. Every time the knife was placed on my body, my thoughts would drift to Ngwa Movawo, how scared he must have been in his last moments here on earth, knowing that he wasn't even guilty of the crimes he was being tortured for, the fear in his eyes knowing that death was approaching.

I wasn't feeling any pain, I don't know why; I must have had an out-of-body experience. Barthelemy would run from a distance and punch my face as the whole room cheered. Ngobese would run from a distance and punch my face. The whole room cheered.

Ndumbe and his girlfriend took turns in spitting and slapping me. People were getting excited, some were even turned on sexually by my torture as I saw Lanna kissing his girlfriend passionately and Ndumbe had Miranda pinned against the wall in a passionate embrace. I thought of my mother and a Bakweri song came to my head with lyrics that said:

> *You did all you did for your children but you died and returned to your maker empty handed.*
> *You are crying but for which of your children are you crying for?*
> *Just pull yourself together.*

Another guy who briefly participated in my torture was Simon, Galina's boyfriend. I met Galina, a beautiful Russian student from Voronezh, while visiting a friend on a different floor. When I left Peter's room Galina followed me. It happened so fast. When we got into the lift she hugged and started kissing me, and instead of going to the third floor, we went to the ninth floor and stopped the lift and engaged in coitus. I had no room, just a sleeping space, so Galina and I used the lift until the lift engineer changed the setting without informing us. While we were engaged in coitus on the ninth floor one day, someone called the lift back to the third floor and we were quite literally caught with our pants down. This was conveyed to Simon. This was the perfect time for him to unleash his revenge. Now he punched me a couple of times and joined the chorus that shouted, 'Kill him and get it over with.'

I was only spared when Jerome busted into the room and said he'd seen some military cars outside the hostel. Some days later I was told that this was a conspiracy between Aubin, Ifeoma the Great and Jerome to free me from the clutches of death. Thankfully it worked. The illegals scattered into their various rooms but when the police didn't turn up Ndumbe came up with the idea of cutting up one of his bed sheets to use as a rope to tie me up.

Ngobese and The Bull went through my small suitcase and found my Cameroonian passport, which was confiscated. I never saw my Cameroonian passport again and I felt stripped of my identity completely. They were looking for my Zimbabwean passport as it would have been worth their while, selling it to the highest bidder. Unfortunately for them I had given my passport to Remy who used it to collect his medication at the local pharmacy. Remy pleaded for these guys to stop the beatings but his pleas, like all others, fell on deaf ears.

At the end of the beating and torture, my hands were tied behind my back, my legs tied by my ankles and knees. I saw certain parts of my body I had not seen before and I was then rolled underneath Ndumbe's bed. I heard Miranda whispering to Lanna saying that they would come and kill me while I was asleep. I never slept. Every time Ndumbe or Miranda woke up to use the toilet they would spit at me and kick me. Ndumbe would use the back of his heel and hit me on the head and other parts of my body; he would throw whatever he could fit into his hands in my direction. In the morning, he poured cold water onto my body; I could not move and the ropes were tight but the water soothed my sores temporarily. I was held hostage by this group of Cameroonians and in this position for three days, only surviving by the water and whatever Jerome and Patrick brought me.

My mouth, jaw and my whole body were in pain. My front canine was broken and, on the spots where the knives had fried my skin, I was developing sores, blisters and ulcers.

On the third day, whilst Ndumbe and his girlfriend Miranda were frolicking in the shower, Jerome, using a pocketknife, opened the door and helped me escape. Jerome was still drunk, his eyes were red, and he would have killed Ndumbe and Miranda if they had come out of that bathroom, he swore, but Jerome is no killer. We were just good children, good boys gone rogue. We did not leave the hostel; Jerome took me to another room, a couple of doors down from Ndumbe's. Fortunately the physical violence ceased, but there was still verbal abuse for the remainder of my time at the hostel.

I must insist, no French Cameroonian took part in this torture, in fact some of them pleaded on my behalf, including one guy we had nicknamed Dr Kumalo. Years later, in 2013, I met Dr Kumalo while working as a bouncer in a bar in Croydon High Street. First, he bumped into me deliberately but did not stop and carried on up the stairs to use the gentlemen's facilities. He turned and briefly we made eye contact; his face looked familiar but I could not remember where I had first seen him. Kumalo was smartly dressed with a brown shirt with the top button opened and a gold cross.

I thought, 'No, this can't be possible.' But as I walked around doing my usual checks, I heard this voice ask, 'Are you Erico?'

The last time someone called me Erico was in Babushkinskaya. I shouted, 'Dr Kumalo.'

He retorted, 'Erico.' We embraced and jumped around, my gosh.

After my shift that evening, we sat down together and drank vodka and reminisced. Kumalo was with his girlfriend and we drank until the early hours. Kumalo told me about the many funerals he attended whilst at Pechatniki, those who never made it.

A couple of days after my escape, the Russian Amon (Russian anti-terror police's rapid response unit) invaded Pechatniki hostel. They wore masks and carried guns. All the doors in the hostel were knocked down and everyone inside was arrested. Pechatniki hostel made the local news, and the *Komsomolskaya Pravda* newspaper described Pechatniki as 'Hell on Earth'. This news report prompted the university to renovate the third floor of Pechatniki. I have heard rumours that people have said that I was the one who had arranged for the Russian Amon to invade the hostel in the early hours of the morning. I'll hold my silence on this.

Chapter 16

The 1998 winter saw me knocking at death's door in Pechatniki, once more. Moscow University ensured the heating was on permanently at the hostel. The snow on the fields that surrounded the campus was deeper than some of us were tall, and everything was painted white as far as the eye could see. The temperatures fell as low as minus 55 degrees according to some news channels and, once again, there were reports of babushkas and dedushkas freezing to death after consuming samagon (homemade vodka) and daring to walk their dogs.

*

I wanted to go back to the mangrove swamps of Tiko, where we used to catch crabs and mud fish. At times the seas were deceptive: first it was a low tide and then, suddenly, it was high tide. I remember Collins one day getting stuck in the mud as the sea was rising, we pulled him out but the sea swallowed his rain boots.

I never caught a single fish using a hook whilst in Mundemba, you could see the mbanga fish in vast numbers swimming up and down the river, some of them wiggled their waist as if mocking our hooks, they were urban fish I guess and had learned a trick or two. No matter what the bait, they simply ignored our hooks; even when we used extra-fattened worms, they would simply munch on the sides of the hook until the worms disappeared.

It wasn't until I got to New Layout in Tiko that I became an expert fisherman. My sister Elizabeth and her husband Mola Paddy relied on me for their fish supply; the river was not very far behind the house, via the cocoa plantation. I also learned and developed the skill of shooting a coconut off the palm from a distance. I would then break the coconut using a flat stone perfectly deposited on the banks of the small river.

One day, as I enjoyed my routine of basking in the sunshine, fishing, and enjoying my coconut, I heard a rustling sound—something was rolling on dried leaves. I saw the water moving in an unnatural pattern then I looked by the pile of coconut shells and saw a huge snake wiggling, slowly. It looked haggard; half its body including the head was inside the water whilst the rest of the snake was striding slowly on the coconut shells. I stood and waited until the snake crossed over to the other side of the river; I then gathered my catch for the day and returned home.

Mola Paddy agreed that I was to never fish in that river again. A couple of weeks later the whole neighbourhood was awakened during the early house of the morning by a very loud shout coming from the direction of the Oben household. We prepared ourselves for the worst news possible. This type of sudden cry only means one thing: there has been a death in the family. Carrying our lamps and torches, we crossed the small rickety bridge, which was on the brink of collapsing, and climbed the small hill to the Oben compound. The sight that greeted us was something straight out of a David Attenborough nature programme. A massive mboma boa constrictor had broken into the family kraal and was in the process of swallowing a goat. The poor goat's head, its front legs and part of its belly were half way down the snake's throat. The snake would have been successful in its mission had it not been for the noisy chickens whom, shocked by what they were witnessing, had formed a chorus and woken up the Oben household and the rest of the neighbourhood.

Both the goat and the boa met an untimely death. A sharp machete was used and the snake was slit open from its mouth all the way down. The goat just fell out. Later that day, parts of the boa and parts of the goat were sent to us for food, but as far as I know, it is still in the freezer. We never touched it. We do not distinguish snakes from the poisonous or non-poisonous, and the goat had gone halfway into

the snake's throat. It would have been rude to refuse the gift from our
neighbours but no one touched them.

*

There were no African gods in Russia and we were alone and left to the elements. On my British Airways flight from Sheremetyevo to Heathrow in July 1999 there was an English pamphlet on the aeroplane and this was its description of Russia. I quote: 'If the daily activities of the people and the skinheads does not kill you, then the horrible weather and extreme cold temperature probably will.' Propaganda maybe, but it has some elements of truth.

We moved in with three others into a one-bedroom house in a quiet suburb in Mytishchi, altogether there were five of us including Jerome and I. We only lasted one night. It was a conspiracy by the landlady and her brother to take money from us and then to chase us out of the house. After all, we were illegal; we didn't have any legs to stand on. After paying four hundred roubles for rent and deposit, the next day the landlady's brother, or so he said he was, came to our new abode with his friends and chased us out of the neighbourhood. He claimed he was in the Russian mafia, but the wrinkles in his face told a different story. He looked like someone who had spent time digging snow in the winter. He was an alcoholic.

If Pechatniki was hell on earth, Rigskayaya market was the place where all labour laws went to die. There was no such thing as Bolshevik communes, all for one and one for all stuff. Rather, it was dog eat dog.

The police/immigration officers had a routine: Mondays, Wednesdays and Fridays were their dedicated days for visiting the market. Like sheep we ran as soon as we saw others running. It was worse in winter as we would climb the fence and wait in the snow until the searches were over. Ninety per cent of those who worked at Rigskayaya market were illegal immigrants, Armenians,

Georgians, Azerbaijanis, Ukrainians, Moldovans, Cameroonians and Nigerians. Rigskayaya was a melting pot of illegal immigrants. As far as I remember, no one was repatriated upon being arrested by immigration officers but when they returned from spending hours at police stations and different detention centres, one thing was certain: all their money would have been taken from them.

Rigskayaya market was not your standard market where you bought single items; it was a massive retail distribution centre for bulk purchases. Truck after truck came and went. If you saw a group of people walking suddenly towards one end of the retail centre, it simply meant they had spotted a truck and that the business owner was looking for people to either help unload or load the truck. People like Ifeoma the Great and Jerome were lucky as they had businessmen they worked for. Though they had no contracts, they were guaranteed at least one hundred roubles to take home. I say take home but the police knew all our routes—those who made it home had developed the techniques of a snow leopard. We would crawl under the barbwire fences and get off the train home two stations before Rigskayaya station.

I was lucky as Remy recommended me to his employer and I was offered a contract, albeit verbally. At first, they paid me eighty roubles but as the Russian rouble was collapsing against the dollar, my earnings were increased to one hundred and twenty and one hundred and fifty roubles a day. I carried my money unevenly across my body: I would hide some under the insole of my shoes, in the many pockets of my trousers and some in my top pocket because police searches normally stopped when money was located. Then it becomes a case of negotiating shtraf (a fine). This was standard and widespread practice.

Remy and I had a set routine for our employers; in the morning we would wash their cars and, in return, when there was an immigration raid, our employers would hide us in the main offices. It was a fair deal. We had half-hour for lunch, after which we loaded and unloaded truck after truck until around eight o'clock.

We had three bosses, all Georgians; two we only saw during immigration raids as we had to go and hide in the office but David, the third boss, oversaw sales, distribution and ensuring that our huge storage always had space. David was always smiling. He was very happy that I spoke Russian, and he would complain to me about the others, how he always had to be with them to monitor and train them continuously.

David was a family man and loved his wife and son dearly. He spoke about them all the time and carried pictures of them. David had met his wife one fine summer's day while walking along the promenade in central Moscow. She had dropped her ice cream on her top and David offered her a handkerchief, their eyes met and the rest was history. I tried this handkerchief technique in London's Green Park one summer's afternoon. The girl told me to: 'Feck off and mind my own business.'

He taught me manual handling and basic first aid, he always made sure I had strong industrial gloves, and he also taught me how to use and drive the pallet trucks. He reminded me of Mola Paddy. Our workplace was specialised in buying and selling in bulk all kinds of detergent. I ran little errands for him including ensuring all letters were posted on time. I washed his car for free and he would bring me homemade Goriatchi Khachapuri, a Georgian delicacy.

David was heartbroken when he found out his wife was having an affair with a Russian police officer. A few weeks later, David was found hanging in the bathroom. The work place was a very sombre place for some months until they employed a Russian dude who, unfortunately, sacked all of us and brought in his own crew instead. This was the last straw; I started planning my exit from Russia again.

As the rouble dropped its value against the dollar, every Tom, Dick and Harry wanted to get involved in buying and selling fake dollars. I was invited to Ivanova to translate for a group of Cameroonians. One of them was a Barondo man from Ndian division where I attended primary school. He was in his late fifties. I cannot remember his name. He was very short and wore oversized clothes, and his head was shaped as if his mother had tried closing her legs when giving birth to him. He told me he knew Mola Paddy but this was a lie—he just wanted me to go along and translate for him. My job was a success but the Barondo man and his guys went behind my back and took five thousand dollars from the client. I didn't know this at the time but this client was someone who had been helping students with immigration authorities in Ivanova.

I loved Jerome very much, and although I thought my life was over, I didn't want to take Jerome down with me. For this reason we started drifting apart. It was deliberate on my part. I was okay with the drift; I knew for a fact that I had one last attempt at leaving Russia and that if I wasn't successful, I was going to kill myself. I had gone to the library in Prospekt Street and in their small English section found a book on suicide. I knew I could go to my friend Aaron's house in Zagarianin and drink a bottle of his homemade vodka along with huge quantities of ibuprofen, sleep myself into a coma, and pass away with no stress.

I had not seen a graveyard in Russia but I knew I had to do a zromelelele—to invoke the spirits of my ancestors and at the same time pay tribute to God for looking after me this far. That evening after saying goodbye to Jerome, who did not ask where I was going, I stopped at the small shop not far from the house and bought a large bottle of vodka. I had to consult with the gods; I had to seek their wisdom. I collected a few bird feathers and tied them with a rubber band (traditionally we use leaves and tree bark) and got on the bus at the main road. I stayed on the bus until we got just outside Mytishchi market and I went to Tania's house, but the neighbours told me they were still on holidays. I crossed the main road, climbed the steps, crossed over Mytishchi Bridge and sat down on the bench and waited for darkness to come.

I removed the bird feathers from my pocket and started walking towards the bridge. The train came and cleared the platform of passengers. This was my cue to start my divinations and incantations. I removed the vodka from my pocket and held the feathers in front of my face and spat on them three times. I then waved them around my head, I touched every joint of my body with the feathers, I called out the name of my father, my paternal grandmother, I called out late Aunty Bae—all the good spirits whose names I could remember. I spat on the feathers again, this time I placed a curse on them, I asked for every evil spirit that had inhabited me to be passed onto the feathers. Once I had finished, I turned my back to the tracks and threw the feathers over my head. I never turned around to look as the cold wind blew the feathers away.

I now entered phase two of the divinations and incantations; I opened the bottle of vodka and with a gentle and subtle voice started chanting an old melodic ritual, a ritual that has been passed down from generations long gone. I called out loud the name of God who resides above all things and asked for peace unto those who no longer reside among us.

Here I was in Russia standing on a train platform and performing a traditional ritual that was handed down to my people over hundreds of years. I was calling my ancestors, I was walking in their footsteps, I was inviting the gods to come and be merry with me in Russia. As I recited, I poured out the bottle of vodka, drop by drop and sometimes in enormous quantities. To balance the equation one must sip straight from the bottle; this pleases the ancestors. By the time the last of the vodka touched the ground I was drunk. The benevolent spirits of my ancestors and the gods themselves had congregated here under a bridge in Mytishchi, a small district to the northeast of Moscow, on the Yauza River. That evening they had drunk with me and they were merry. They had danced with me, they had accepted my sacrifice, they had cleansed my path. In my heightened state of trance and hallucination, I saw a cluster of bats coming my direction that had human heads. I smiled, the gods were now with me; they were effectively acting on my behalf. I was at peace with myself, reassured. I knew they would not fail me.

High as a kite I jumped on the southbound train and went to my friend's house in Zagarianin, where I would spend my last days in Russia blackening white paper with iodine to the value of two thousand, seven hundred dollars. The rest, which brought the total to three thousand dollars, were real American dollars. Once I had completed the bundle, I left Zagarianin heading for Ivanovo Gorod Nevesta.

Throughout this period, I spent my free time with Dima my half-Russian, half-Armenian girlfriend who lived in Lublino, two stops from Pechatniki. Dima would visit me in Mytishchi on Saturdays and stayed until the Monday. She was my Princess Dima and I was her Prince Charles. We would have picnics in fields of yellow summer flowers; we spent most weekends together apart from when I started dating Tania, a girl I had met in Mytishchi market. Just before Tania went away with her parents for their summer holidays to St Petersburg, she came to our house and informed me that she was pregnant. As I write these memoirs, I could have an eighteen-year-old son or daughter around Mytishchi somewhere.

Chapter 17

I remember very well—it was coming up May and summer was at its peak—that before making my way to Ivanovo, I decided to make a quick stop at the hostel in Pechatniki to pay another fifty dollars to Ndumbe. At the hostel, I met an English Cameroonian called Kattooh. I had heard about this guy a lot in Cameroon, he was many years older than me and like Ifoma, was a prolific footballer. I attended the same high school in Buea where Kattooh had mastered his trade as a footballer. He agreed to accompany me to Ivanovo despite people's warnings; telling him I was an ill omen, a descendant from the devil himself. Despite this warning, Kattooh never judged me and followed me to Ivanovo on his own accord.

I bought Kattooh and I some new clothes, branded Nike T-shirts and trainers. We looked summery; a little bit business-like but not too serious. Kattooh was worried about this contract he had entered into with me, the devil. He would say things like 'Erico, if you do anything, if you scam me, I will kill you.'

I listened without really paying any attention. Ivanovo is about two hundred and sixty kilometres away, about six hours' journey but with those rickety communist buses, the journey went on and on. The bus always stopped somewhere halfway into the journey for passengers to stretch their legs and have some food. In Ivanovo, Kattooh and I went to a student hostel. Jay-Jay was always very happy to see me and that evening I entertained the whole hostel with drinks while Jerome supplied plenty of pepper soup. I was so tempted to tell Jerome what my mission in Ivanovo was but he had become that close to me, I couldn't put him in harm's way. I did not confide in Jerome, but I knew he knew what my mission was in Ivanovo.

The first couple of days I scouted around the hostel area looking for clients or potential victims. I visited several markets and wherever I went, Kattooh followed me. I really did not need Kattooh—he had no role to play in the business. I was now the translator and the business head; I had all the goods and knew how to provide the service. I just wanted Kattooh to be my witness in case I ended up being killed.

On the third day we wandered out of our comfort zone and entered an unknown territory. After walking for ages and almost giving up, we came across a café; this was a good sign, so we went in for some breakfast. We had some tea and an assortment of cold meats and Kattooh told me about his footballing heydays. I had heard about Kattooh and his footballing skills but right here right now in Ivanova, his reverie and nostalgia were more like noise in my ears. At this stage my mind had already left Russia, I was in Bulawayo somewhere, hitchhiking my way back to Cameroon.

'How will my mother greet me?' My mind would wonder. Would it be with a kiss, a tight hug, or with a slap asking how the heck I ended up in Russia? Knowing my mother, it would have been with a slap to the back of my head. I also wondered how would she react if I told her I had become an outright sinner? A scammer? I was an Ibo Nigerian. I was now an official graduate from the school of Boy Boy.

*

I remember when my sister Elizabeth became pregnant with her first child, Ngalle Collins Kulu. My mother went ballistic. My sister was in form three in one of the poshest girls' boarding schools in the country—Saker Baptist College. Effectively, my sister could not continue her education, and when she found out who was responsible for my sister's pregnancy, Mola Nganeli, my mother marched right to their college. At the time Mola Nganeli attended one of the poshest boys' schools in the country—St Joseph's College Sasse. If my mother were successful in reporting Nganeli to the college principal, it would have meant an instant dismissal from the school. At the entrance to the college, her brother, Uncle Evella, who at the time was a lecturer at this college, met my mother. (Uncle Evella is a doctor in America now and has been selected as the chief of our village, which has created a schism amongst our different tribesmen.)

Fortunately, Uncle Evella's intervention saved Nganeli and he was able to complete his studies and become one of the big sharks in Sonara Limbe's petrol chemical plant.

My mother's reputation preceded her; that is why the mention of her name sends quivers down some of the villagers' spines. It was because of her reputation that some of the villagers mocked her for standing up for me and against my father's family. It was because of her reputation that my father's family had rejected her and in so doing rejected me.

*

We were at the restaurant for almost an hour before a middle-aged gentleman, dressed in white shirt and black trousers, with perfectly polished black shoes, walked into the restaurant. I can't remember his name but he dragged a chair over and sat at our table and ordered some more tea for us. He spoke very gently and told us he was the owner of the restaurant.

Next, he opened his man bag and showed us the contents: a huge quantity of cocaine. He said it carried the street value of ten thousand dollars.

He asked, 'Where are you guys from?'

I told him we were from Moscow and he wanted to know what we were doing in Ivanovo. This was my cue to sell him the idea of the reproductive dollars business.

I told him my name was Ocimile Majola Thambvani and that I was an attaché to the American Embassy, and that I was looking for businessmen in Ivanovo who were interested in the buying and selling of dollars. The guy's ears were as rigid as a lioness moving incognito towards her prey. Once I knew I had got his attention, I carried on with the rehearsed lines, 'America is flooding the Russian market with dollars in order to render the rouble useless.' This convinced him that I must have inside information.

He looked around and asked, 'Are you police officers or something?'

I replied, 'No, we are not police officers. We are just businessmen.'

He left his chair and went outside for a few minutes. When he returned, we continued our small meeting in a room in the back of the restaurant. I was made to repeat everything I had told him about the business. The gentleman could not believe his ears; he said he had heard of such businesses and he himself was worried about the continuous flooding of the Russian market with the dollars. I told him I had around fifteen thousand dollars' worth, all in its original form; the only thing missing was the chemical so I could restore the dollars into exchangeable currency. The guy could not believe what he was hearing, he said if this was possible, he would give up his drug-selling business and invest in our transactions instead.

I told him, with an investment of five thousand dollars, he would have a one hundred per cent return. He asked where we lived and I told him we had been staying in Ivanovo for a week and that we were returning to Moscow the next day.

He said, 'Don't worry guys, I will find you a room to stay and we shall do some business.' The client then took us to a beautiful one-bedroom flat somewhere in Ivanovo. He promised to pick us up in the morning for a drive to Moscow to collect the pre-prepared bundles of dollars I had left in Zagarianin.

In our new flat, I had to repeat again to Kattooh everything that had taken place; Kattooh was excited but again repeated his warning about me not scamming him. For what it was worth, I told Kattooh we would split any money we made fifty-fifty.

The client came very early the next morning. He was with

162

another guy whom we didn't recognise, and woke us up saying, 'Let's go, we're off to Moscow.'

It was the first time I had seen a BMW that was all black with tinted windows. We got in and drove at full speed to Moscow. Having arrived in Kiyevskaya, they parked the car across the road from the Diplomatic Corpus, where they waited for me. I jumped on a northbound train until I got to Komsomolskaya, and from there I took the overground train to Zagarianin.

Aaron was a bit surprised to see me; I told him I was just passing through and he left me to my own devices. Inside my room I separated the three hundred iodine-stained dollars and sealed the rest of the bundles as perfectly as possible. I then placed fairy liquid in two different medical bottles and sealed them with tape, writing chemical elements on the sides of each bottle that even Sheldon, the physicist in *The Big Bang Theory*, would have struggled to understand. I placed all the contents into my bag.

Once I was ready, I begged Aaron's friend for a lift to Zagarianin station, where I reversed my journey to Kiyevskaya and re-joined Kattooh and the client. I flashed the client the well-sealed bundle. I had told Kattooh that the only time we spoke in Pidgin English was away from the client so all through this journey Kattooh was quiet unless I asked express permission from the client to translate for Kattooh. This was all part of my plan, as I could not allow any room for doubt. When we arrived back in Ivanovo I asked the client to buy some gloves and syringes from the pharmacy and he did so without any hesitation. When we got back to the house the client and his friend ordered some food and vodka, then he handed me a hundred-dollar bill and I started the process.

I removed two dollar-sized papers from the package and gently placed the client's one hundred dollars in the middle, forming a sandwich. I then sealed it exactly like the one I was carrying in my jacket pocket. Once it was sealed, I put on my pair of gloves and, using the syringe, injected the chemicals into the package. I then asked the client to put on a pair of gloves and place the bundle inside the freezer. I did the injecting and replacing in the freezer every hour and by the third hour I had swapped the new package with the one I was carrying in my jacket pocket.

We drank vodka and ate smoked fish. I then placed the sealed package between two books, wrapped it tight and handed the bundle to the client to take home, telling him, 'It must be kept in the freezer.'

The next day at around nine in the morning the client and his friend came to the house prepared to see a miracle. We formed a circle in the living room and I brought in a bowl of warm water then I put on my gloves and proceeded to use the syringe to withdraw some chemicals from my well-labelled containers. I then carefully placed the iodine-stained dollars into the bowl. Their faces lit up when the iodine vaporised as I gently shook the bowl from left to right. It was a miracle. My face betrayed no emotion, the clients' mouths were agape, even Kattooh was impressed.

I then asked Kattooh to bring in the ironing board and once the last of the dollars had been ironed, I quickly carried the bowl of washing liquid and disposed of it in the toilet.

People have said that I sold Kattooh to the devil but I did not: this is my account of what happened and it is the truth. When the clients came to see us that evening, they told us about their experience at the money exchange—how the person at the exchange had checked and re-checked the stains on the dollar, and this only served to increase their curiosity and interest in the scam. They told us how they had been asked if the dollars were homemade.

The clients had promised to pick us up at the house early in the morning for a trip to Moscow to collect three thousand dollars' worth of chemicals. I was happy; we were on the brink of making three thousand dollars. I had already agreed with Kattooh on a fifty-fifty split but as we were only going to have three thousand dollars, I was starting to think that maybe I should only offer Kattooh one thousand dollars—after all, he had done nothing, he was just company. Also, how was I going to separate from Kattooh and meet up later to divide the loot? I knew there was no way they would hand over three thousand dollars to us and just wait in their car while we went to purchase the so-called chemicals, one of us had to stay back as collateral.

From the house the clients took us to watch an opera about a young man who was stuck in hell because of his brown skin and dark hair. The clients were laughing, 'Oh, they killed a black man for no reason.'

To cheer us up after the depressing opera, the clients took us to a nightclub where we danced and drank. At around eleven in the evening, the client and his friend said goodbye and left, while Kattooh and I stayed at the club until about one in the morning. We had been drinking and chatting with two girls the clients had introduced us to and at the end of the night, the girls joined us in a taxi headed to our abode. We never made it to the house for as soon as we left the high street, we were stopped by armed police officers; the girls were separated from us while Kattooh and I were taken to the police station somewhere in Ivanovo.

I protested, 'Do you know who I am? I am a Zimbabwean diplomat, if you do not free me, it will be a diplomatic crisis.' I nagged and nagged. The young guard eventually became fed up and around three in the morning, he checked my status document, which was a laminated photocopy of my Zimbabwean passport with a stamp from Ivan Ivanovic Locev, head of Russia's third immigration district.

I knew that I was legal, albeit not in Ivanovo. The young guard authorised my release but said they could not release Kattooh until his documents were checked and this could only be done after nine in the morning, once the guards had been changed. Kattooh insisted his passport was at the student hostel in Ivanovo, which could only be retrieved in the morning.

I returned to the flat but I could not sleep. When the clients arrived in the morning to pick us up, I told them what had happened. This almost derailed the whole programme for the clients were miffed; they asked that if Kattooh was a diplomat like me, how come he had not been released? I told them whilst I was carrying my documents, Kattooh had left his at the embassy. They were not going to risk going to the police station because of their involvement with cocaine; instead we took on the six hours' drive from Ivanovo to Moscow.

We drove into Kiyevskaya where the clients parked their car across the road from the Diplomatic Corpus. I was then handed a carrier bag with three thousand dollars in one-hundred-dollar bills. According to the clients, I was to use this money to get enough chemicals to produce nine thousand dollars.

The clients warned me, 'Listen, if you fuck with us, we will kill you and your friend.'

'Don't worry my friends, everything will be just fine,' I said and placed the money into my man bag and told the clients I would be back in around ninety minutes. My heart had never beaten faster as I walked away from the black tinted BMW. I crossed the road, and turned left at the gates of the Diplomatic Corpus. My brain was telling me to start running but I couldn't. I had three thousand dollars on me, in central Moscow: my heart pounded.

I walked past the attaché to the British Embassy in Kiyevskaya, I walked past Kiyevskaya overground station and looked to see if Sasha was there. I saw two police officers, with their huge German Shepherds, carrying Kalashnikovs. One of them was the young guy who had stopped me previously and spoken to me a couple of times whilst I was a temporary resident at the station. This was the time for them to stop and search me, I thought to myself. Instead, they waved at me; it was as if the gods had mysteriously whispered something into their ears.

As I disappeared in the crowded underground station, I remembered my rites of passage as a twelve-year-old wrestler and saw the metaphor of that black boy, who had painted his face black and reddened his eyes with extract from a plant; the black boy who had failed to master the secrets of the Palapala fight, the black boy who thought brute force was the order of the day, the black boy who exiled himself from the village after the molikilikili had brought him down, the black boy shunned, stunned and decapitated by the curse of patriarchy.

It was June 1999—two years and one month since I had arrived in Russia.

I had moved from being an illegal Cameroonian to being a legal Zimbabwean. I knew the skills and the routine of human traffickers, and I knew how to perform dollar scams. I walked and wondered how long it would take for the clients to realise what had happened, that they had been scammed. What was going to happen to Kattooh? Was he still at the police station in Ivanovo? Had he left the police station? Was he still in Ivanovo? Was he en route to Moscow? Whatever it was, I knew I had eight hours in Moscow before I disappeared. If anyone was following me or monitoring my movements they would have known that I was up to no good. My brain was thinking faster than my legs, so much so that when I got to the escalators at Arbatskaya Station, instead of using the outbound escalators, I struggled to use the inbound escalators. My brain could not register or understand why I was unable to go up out of the station. To the left of me I could clearly see people standing comfortably, lovers kissing and using the appropriate escalators. My brain had frozen. This was the case until a babushka took my hand and directed me towards the outbound escalators. Under her breath I heard her say, 'Poor black boy, his brain is not enough.' I was behaving like a coconut, I was there and not there at the same time. As she walked away, I shouted, 'Thank you very much.' She just shook her head.

'Good afternoon Sir, how can I help you?' asked Ella from behind the glass counter. She looked bored.

'Can I have a plane ticket to Zimbabwe?' I didn't know the communication etiquette nor the necessities like please and thank you. Sour conversation continued with a tense vibe; Ella thought

I was being rude, I thought she was being rude. She clicked and clicked without looking at me.

She then asked, 'Can I see your passport please?'

I handed over my laminated Zimbabwean passport without saying a word. She glanced at it and then looked at me and continued clicking. I was wowed by how fast she was typing.

'Are you Russian?' I asked. She pushed her glasses towards the front end of her nose and looked up at me and said, 'No, I am from England, a place called Thornton Heath.'

She said she'd only been working for British Airlines for three months and she was dreading the winter. Then she said, 'Mr Ocimile, the nearest departure date for Zimbabwe is the 29th of July and the ticket will cost you one million roubles.'

The date meant I would have to wait a month but beggars can't be choosers. I would just have to try my best to lay low until my day of salvation arrived.

'How much is that in dollars?' I asked. Ella then clicked and clicked and a few minutes later said, 'One thousand two hundred dollars.'

I placed my man bag on the counter, reached into it and pulled out the three thousand dollars. This was the first time I heard the word 'blimey'. I counted out and handed over one thousand two hundred dollars to Ella. She counted it again, just to be on the safe side and then clicked and clicked and I heard a printer spring to life. Ella then handed me my ticket saying, 'Remember, this ticket is non-refundable.'

I was to travel to Zimbabwe on the 29th of July 1999. My flight path was Moscow Sheremetyevo via London Heathrow via Johannesburg South Africa, arriving in Harare in Zimbabwe. Ella then advised me that a fee would be charged if I were to change my travel date but I had no intention of changing my travel date.

She ended the conversation by saying, 'Have a safe journey Mr Ocimile and enjoy your flight.'

I asked Ella if she would like to have a drink with me later, she smiled but politely declined. When I was working in Croydon and living in Brixton, every time bus 250 or 109 went past to Thornton Heath, it reminded me of Ella.

With my ticket safe in my pocket, I travelled to Textilshiki station where I stopped at a liquor store and bought two bottles of Standard Russian Vodka and three boxes of Russian chocolates. The guard in the reception at the police station searched me. It was just a formality now, they were used to me coming and going. He knew I was there to see the head of immigration. He asked if he could have a bottle of vodka, I smiled and offered it to him as I had anticipated such an event. Upstairs, I showed the head of immigration my flight ticket and handed him the vodka and said, 'Thank you very much Sir.'

He replied, 'You are welcome.' He then said something that caught me completely off guard, 'So please tell me, what is your date of birth?'

I could not remember my own date of birth. I mumbled pretending not to know the right words. The head of immigration called his secretary and asked her to renew my exit visa. When she left, he said, 'Look, please do not return to my office or I will put you in jail.'

I handed the chocolates to the two secretaries, we chatted for a while, then I tried my boldest move ever, I asked the younger of the two if it would be possible for her to accompany me to the airport and ensure I got onto the aeroplane. She said the head of immigration could only sanction such a mission. We chatted briefly as I said goodbye dreading the possibility of not being able to make it through the airport. Fortunately the secretary followed me until we were outside of the station. For a fee of three hundred dollars, she would ensure me a safe passage out of Russia. This was the best news. I agreed to her proposal and we shook hands. Then I reached into my man bag and handed her one hundred dollars and we agreed I would pay the rest once we were at the airport. She gave me her direct telephone number. We hugged and she said, 'See you soon.'

I departed and went to see the rector and ask him for some invitation letters. After all, I too could become a human trafficker I thought. I went to Lublino and picked up Dima, and together we went to Pechatniki where I paid the rest of Ndumbe's money. I even gave two hundred roubles to another Bakossi guy who had just been released from prison for selling cocaine. A few murmurs were made, people enquired about Kattooh and I said he was still in Ivanovo. From Pechatniki, I took Dima to Okhotny Ryad in central Moscow where we shopped for new clothes for her and myself, then we had a three-course dinner. In my heart of hearts I knew this was going to be our last supper as a couple. We kissed in the streets of central Moscow then visited GUM shopping mall in central Moscow, which is just a stone's throw away from the Kremlin. I asked if she would like to come to Africa with me, her eyes lit up and she said it would be a dream-come-true.

I knew that the first place Kattooh would look for me, if he made it to Moscow, would be Dima's house, so while I enjoyed her company, I was conscious of time.

From Okhotny Ryad, Dima and I visited the rest of the illegals, who still had jobs in Rigskayaya market, including Jerome. I bought all of them shaslik (barbecued meat roasted on site) without telling anyone where I had been or where I was going.

The clients were probably still waiting for me at Kiyevskaya station, either that or the police would have approached and asked them to move on. Black-haired Russians in a tinted car, across the road from the diplomatic corpus in Kiyevskaya, would attract police attention. When I dropped Dima home, I caught the train to Komsomolskaya, and from there I travelled to Zagarianin, where I lived with Aaron and his family, counting the days down until my departure from Russia.

Chapter 18

I was shocked when, while the young children were asleep and we were drinking in the living room, Aaron brought out some syringes and started injecting himself with gheroine, as they call it in Russia. His eyes rolled in his head and he went into a state of complete silence, I mean he was like an ekongi, a ghost. Aaron loved the good life. I would give him two hundred dollars for allowing me to conduct my business from the family home, and when he'd spent the money, he would ask for more. Every time this happened, I would tell him I had to go and collect it from the embassy; I didn't want him to know I had money in my brief case and my man bag. Aaron also liked playing the slot machines in the casinos. He dreamt of riches and wealth, but that was all it was, a dream. He too had been sacked from his job at Rigskayaya market and now he was involved in small buying and selling in Zagarianin market, mostly fresh vegetables. He had made friends with another Armenian guy and they owned a small stall. When Aaron asked where I was going all packed, I said I was going to visit a friend in Ivanovo. I could not bring myself to tell him I would never see him again.

That evening, I caught the train from Zagarianin to Komsomolskaya and from there I caught a south bound train stopping at Lublino. When Dima saw me, the first thing she said was that Kattooh had been there to look for me. I asked if he had been alone and she said he was. For me this meant one of two things—that Kattooh had successfully left Ivanova or the clients bailed him out and brought him back to Moscow to look for me. That evening I took Dima and her family out for a meal so they didn't have to cook and also bought her father a big bottle of champagne. We always slept in different rooms when I stayed at

171

Dima's house and tonight was not going to be any different. Maybe if I had confided in her that I would never see her again, it would have been different.

I left Dima's house when the whole family were asleep. On my pillow was a note with one hundred dollars. On the note were these words: 'I love you my queen, but I must go home, do not forget about me.'

When I reached the back of the building the immigration officer was already there but she was not alone, she had brought her sister, who was even more beautiful, with her. Together we caught the train to Belorusskaya station and from there we caught the direct bus to Sheremetyevo Moscow International Airport.

As we walked towards the airport's entrance, the immigration officer asked me to hand over the rest of the money to her sister, then she went into the airport and confirmed the flight. She told me I had to wait until every other passenger had checked in. I was having an out-of-body experience. Was I going to pull this off? My Zimbabwean passport photo showed an older person, anybody with eyes would recognise straight away that it wasn't me. I waited with the sister, I was not sure what the immigration officer was doing, but she was inside the airport area. Then, around an hour later, she came out and beckoned me over. At first, we walked past the check in, and I wasn't asked any questions, then the passport control; again no questions. In fact I went through the whole airport without a single spot check, and eventually I walked into what felt like a tarpaulin that lead directly into the aeroplane. I could not believe what was happening. The immigration officer was slightly ahead of me and asked me to walk a bit faster. I could see some of the flight attendants waiting for me at the entrance of the aeroplane.

I was greeted with, 'Good afternoon Sir, welcome aboard British Airways.' I was the last passenger to board the aeroplane. The immigration officer hugged me and asked if I still had her telephone number. She then said, 'Safe journey, and please do call me when you arrive in Zimbabwe.'

She cried. It was only later after telephoning Misha, yes, her name is Misha, from my flat in Grangetown in Cardiff that she told me that she had been in love with me all that time.

I sat on the left side of the aeroplane, next to the window, and until I heard the announcement that the aeroplane was about to take off, I still could not believe what was happening. There was an announcement for us to put our seatbelts on. I heard the engines roar and the aeroplane jerk forward. The next time I looked out in the window, the aeroplane was in the air, in full flight. There was a small lump growing in my throat and I swallowed; it didn't matter if anyone was looking at me, I cried and my tears were visible.

'Are you okay, Sir?' One of the airhostesses noticed I was crying.

'Yes, I'm just afraid of flying,' I said.

She asked if I wanted anything to drink and when I replied yes, she brought me two small glasses of wine. She asked if I was hungry. When I answered in the affirmative, she brought me two chicken legs, some carrots and sprouts. I fell asleep after drinking my wine and finishing my meal and dreamt about the story we were told as children, as to why the millipede has no ears.

*

Every time the millipede passed a house on his way to the market, he saw the molikilikili with his skinny arms and legs on the trunk of the Iroko tree, trying to push it over. This happened many times so one day the millipede decided to stop and ask the molikilikili what it was trying to achieve by pushing the Iroko tree. The molikilikili responded by saying, 'This Iroko tree is blocking the sunlight into my house, so I intend to push it until it falls.'

The millipede said, 'Can I bring to your attention the sheer size of this tree?' The molikilikili replied, 'I have time, I will push until it falls.'

The millipede then prayed to the gods saying, 'Please gods, remove

my ears, I do not wish to hear what the molikilikili is saying.' The
gods granted his wish and hence he lost his ears. To this day, the
molikilikili still pushes believing he will bring down the Iroko tree
one day. Unlike the molikilikili, I have been successful in leaving
Russia under bizarre circumstances.

*

When I woke up, the aeroplane was arriving at London Heathrow.
I looked out the window and saw the Corpthorne Hotel and in
the distance, beautifully tall buildings. I had arrived in England. I
was now trespassing the land of the people who colonised and
forgot me; who brought Shakespeare, *Silas Marner*, Chaucer and
Father Francis, who had baptised and changed my name to Eric
Charles. I was now in the land of the people whose legacy in my
village is one of corrugated iron roofs. I was now transiting in the
Land of Milk and Honey, the land where being a citizen places one
at the front of the queue in the lottery of life, the land of the Great
William Wilberforce who died only three days after the passing
of the Slavery Abolition Act 1883.

When the aeroplane came to its final stop at the terminal and
the passengers started exiting, a bulky gentleman came and stood
next to me saying, 'Please Mr Ocimile, wait until all the other
passengers have left the aeroplane, I will then take you to the
departure lounge for your connecting flight.'

I waited patiently and once the aeroplane was empty, the bulky
man led me out into the terminal building. We walked along long,
clean and crystal white corridors and through the windows I could
see different aeroplanes landing and taking off. We walked until
we arrived at a room with thirty or so white women in their late
sixties or seventies. The gentleman said. 'Mr Ocimile, please wait
here until you hear the announcement for your connecting flight
to Johannesburg, South Africa.'

I sat down and watched these women knitting.

*

I thought of my mother and the kind of web she must have weaved, the kind of dances she must have performed. What kind of mating ritual did my mother do in order to get involved with the kind of men who ensured her children were born?

Apart from my elder sister Elizabeth and third sister, Ndinge, whose fathers I never met, I remember them. I remember my sister, Christina—my mother's second daughter—whose father was a traditional doctor from the village of Bokwango at the foot of Mount Cameroon. I remember going to his house when we were small but after that visit I promised never ever to go back there. He was a loser whatever barometer you used, yet somehow my sister was born.

Then there was Krimau's father, a distant relative of the Kai family from our village. When I met him, he was dishevelled and on his last legs. Then there was Motakori, Queenta's father, who hailed from the Barondo clan and did some sort of cleaning or clerical job at Buea General Hospital.

As for me, I was too young to remember meeting my father and until this day I have not seen a photograph of him. My mother told me recently, after his death, his family destroyed all memory of him. When I went to the printing press office where he worked, all his things had been given to members of his family, including photographs, which were nowhere to be found. Were their actions deliberate? I do not know and in fact I dread to think. I just went with what the villagers, especially Mola Etonge and Chief Efange, told me about him.

I heard during the court case that, apparently, I walked like my father and I looked and talked like my father. Although my mother attested to the perfect love they had for one another, her history with other men was something my father's family despised, and this judgment against my mother and her character was their motive to dragging her through the courts and challenging my father's will. Two years before the court case, she started seeing an Ibo man, from Small

Soppo, called Pa Joe. This man was married, he had two wives and around eight children and I thought to myself, 'Seriously? You already have two wives who lived side-by-side in a tiny wooden house.'

I didn't mind though because every time Pa Joe visited my mother's house he would bring her a bunch of plantains and he always ensured I had money so I could go out and entertain my friends. As a matter of fact, I take my hat off to Pa Joe; he supported my mother all through the court case and spent time consoling her when we eventually lost the case.

One thing is for certain: though the fathers never actively took part in helping my mother bring up their children, they ensured we carried their characteristic in our genes.

For all her frailties, Iya Sarah Efeti Kange is one iron lady; I for one have modelled my life on the knowledge she imparted to me. She never took any rubbish from the men who came and went out of her life. I nicknamed her the black widow spider—never to her face though or else I run the risk of getting smacked!

*

As the time dragged on inside the lounge at Heathrow airport, one of the women, the oldest among them, began looking at me intensely. Every time I looked back at her, she would bend her head and pay attention to her knitting. Then, with an accent that I only heard again when I started working for Lilywhites in Piccadilly Circus, she said, 'Excuse me boy, where are you coming from?'

'Russia,' I replied.

She shook her whole body as if she was freezing and said, 'It must have been really cold for you boy.' She carried on without allowing me to answer and said they were going back to 'Jo Burg' before adding that Jo Burg was short for Johannesburg. By this point all the other women had stopped their knitting and were paying attention to our conversation.

'So, where's your destination?' she asked.

I answered 'Bulawayo' and she looked at her friends and said. 'We don't like Mugabe do we girls?' She carried on talking about their time in Germany and how they were going hunting in South Africa.

I started to feel apprehensive about going to South Africa. After all, it had only been nine years since apartheid had collapsed and the way she was calling me boy, she looked as if she was in deep reminiscence of the good old days. I had read about South Africa and had developed an unconscious bias or maybe a small hatred for white South Africans. She wouldn't stop talking and said how she had a couple of good-looking boys like me, whom she employed. I thought maybe these were part of the one per cent of whites who owned ninety-nine per cent of South Africa's wealth. She said her name was Brunilda. I pretended I was dozing off. I yawned and stretched—she got the hint and stopped talking.

Chapter 19

The whole village was brought to a standstill one morning when loud cries rang from every household—the day Rudi's mother died. Aunty Kwashi was the politest, the friendliest and the warmest woman. She would never pass without greeting you, she had the biggest smile and was amongst the very few in the village who called me OC after my father Oscar. The whole village cried and we held vigils and sang melodies and eulogies to Aunty Kwashi. After this, Rudi and I became very close. I used to borrow his shirts and cravats. I spent most of my free time with Rudi and we would go for long walks and enjoyed reading books. Every time we met, we would deconstruct books and dream of lands far away.

*

I remembered my last conversation with Rudi; he told me about his relatives who had come to Great Britain. Rudi dreamt of crossing Heathrow International Airport. He dreamt of leaving Cameroon behind and said he would remove his shoes at Heathrow and shake out the dust of Cameroon. I remember us talking about the kings and queens of Great Britain, those ordained by God. I remember the famous lines by Old John of Gaunt, 'This royal throne of kings, this scepter'd isle, this earth of majesty, this seat of Mars, this other Eden and demi-paradise.'

I was sat at the departure lounge of Heathrow airport waiting for my flight to Jo Burg and then another flight to Harare in Zimbabwe, where I ran the risk of being arrested and locked up for impersonating Mr Ocimile. I remembered when I was negotiating the purchase of that passport from Vincent he had told me the number of countries this passport could be used for entry to without a visa, and one of them was Great Britain. I sat there and started thinking—maybe I should try and see if I could enter Great Britain as a Zimbabwean. What was the worst thing that could happen? I would be refused entry, I would then go back to the departure lounge and wait for my flight to Johannesburg. One thing was certain—they were not going to return me to Russia.

As I pondered, as my mind played with indecisiveness, an official came to tell us our flight had been delayed and as he was about to leave, I asked him if it was possible for me to see an immigration officer? Now I did not know about becoming an asylum seeker, let alone a refugee. Asylum seekers and refugees for me were Namibians and South Africans that had fled to Cameroon during the height of apartheid. My mother had hosted around five Namibians, and their stories were harrowing. The official said no problem and took me downstairs to the arrivals desk where I was introduced to Mr Marlow, an immigration officer.

'How can I help you?' Mr Marlowe asked me. In my thick Cameroonian accent I said, 'I want to come to the UK for a visit.'

I handed over my passport to him. Mr Marlowe looked at the passport, then he looked at me, he looked at the passport again then he looked back at me. He then placed the passport under a machine that moved back and forth whilst at the same time flashing a ray of blue light. Mr Marlowe did this repeatedly, then he disappeared into a room and after around ten minutes I could see something like five pairs of eyes looking directly at me through the glass. I was panicking—thinking they must have discovered I was not the person in that passport and summoned the international police to come and arrest me.

'So where have you travelled from?' Mr Marlowe asked.

'I just came from Russia,' I said.

'What is your destination?'

179

'Harare,' I said.

'So why do you want to stop over in the United Kingdom? Have you got any friends in the United Kingdom?'

'Yes.' I said.

'Where are your friends?' Mr Marlowe asked.

I remembered the Corpthorne Hotel that I saw when the aeroplane was touching down, so I just blurted out, 'Yes. My friends are in Corpthorne Hotel.'

Mr Marlowe then requested my suitcase, which he searched thoroughly, before disappearing again with my passport into the small room. Just a few yards away from me I could see families greeting their family members who had arrived from some corner of the earth. I was at Heathrow airport trying to make a daring entry into the United Kingdom. I had been successful in leaving Russia with a Zimbabwean passport, but there was no way I was going to pull this off, not with the sophistication of the United Kingdom's technology.

Mr Marlowe returned with more questions.

'Where in Zimbabwe are you from then, Mr Ocimile?'

'Bulawayo,' I replied.

We were there for ages before, eventually, Mr Marlowe asked if I had any money. I reached into my man bag and pulled out eight hundred dollars and a few hundred roubles.

Then Mr Marlowe said, 'Mr Ocimile, could you please sign your signature on this piece of paper?'

I had anticipated this question and had memorised the signature just in case I had such difficulties in Johannesburg or in Harare. Mr Marlowe handed me a pen and I scribbled a replica of the signature that was in my Zimbabwean passport, authenticating me as Mr Ocimile Marjola Thambvani.

Mr Marlowe then stamped my passport with a six months' entry visa and said. 'Mr Ocimile, welcome into the UK. Just remember, you are not allowed to work.'

He then handed me my passport and showed me through to

the arrival lounge. At first, I walked slowly, and then my heart started pounding again. I had gone through two of the most powerful airports on earth; I had gone through immigration authorities in two nuclear powerhouses. I remembered when I threw a stone in the direction of the monitor lizard. Today it wasn't shaking its head and laughing at me mockingly. Instead, I had the last laugh.

I went to the money exchange at the airport and exchanged two hundred dollars and I was sure that lady scammed me, for she handed me over something like one hundred pounds. I asked her for some coins, as I wanted to use the telephone.

Sister Ndinge was excited to hear my voice. She was my mirror; when she died my life was plunged into another extreme.

I was starving but I had developed a linguistic inferiority complex. I walked towards a café and there were cakes, croissants and sandwiches (I had not heard the word sandwich before) and I waited for the people in front of me to place their orders but I had difficulties understanding their accents. When it was my turn to order, the only words that came out of my mouth were, 'Can I have a coffee?'

The girl retorted with, 'Would you like black or white coffee?'

I looked at her thinking such questions were only asked in South Africa. My god it was boiling hot and there was no sugar in it. I didn't know that once you had bought the coffee, there was another section on the corner for sugar and other condiments. I was a proper, what we call in my village, Johnny Just Come. I was a jungle man in Heathrow.

The coffee tasted horrible. As I walked back towards the main entrance, that was when I saw it, a National Express bus. And not just any National Express Bus—this one had a sign that said Swansea via Cardiff.

Let me explain to you the significance of this Swansea via Cardiff sign. I was attracted to the imagery of the name Swansea but that was not the name that captured my interest and my imagination. You see in 1990, when the whole of Cameroon and my village still suffered from the PTSD of losing against England at the quarter finals of the 1990 World Cup, Mola Francis had just returned to the village from studying abroad.

I remembered us playing football at the Ajax Maija ma' Ngowa's stadium and during the short intervals we would sit around Mola Francis as he told us about his escapades abroad. He studied mathematics at Cardiff University, (Mola Francis is actually now a mathematics teacher at Fitzalan High School in Cardiff) and the things he kept talking about were the beautiful skies of Cardiff and the daffodils of Swansea; he spoke about how great Cardiff University was for academics and research. He spoke at length about how graceful and accommodating the people of Wales were; we dreamed of walking in his shoes. Mola Francis is a brainbox from St Joseph's College Sasse, and he had won a government scholarship that saw him studying in and eventually settling in Wales. Listening to him talking about Wales meant we created all kinds of utopias in our heads—there was no way there could be a place, a country, a people with such perfection.

Mola Francis showed us leaflets about studying and living in Wales, he showed us leaflets about the Brecon Beacons, how the landscape of Wales was very similar to that of Buea—there were hills and mountains. He showed us leaflets on different educational institutions of Wales but the fees were so exorbitant that the whole of my family would have had to work for fifty years just to pay for one year of studies.

Now here I was standing outside Heathrow airport, looking at a bus that had a sign saying Swansea via Cardiff. I looked around me and saw a small group of people smoking cigarettes, there were no police officers with dogs or Kalashnikovs, there were no red-eyed black men and women waiting for their prey, there were no barons, no false promises of a transit. I had arrived in a perfect land, a place where the laws of human existence are upheld. On top of the mountain I could see a pot of gold, all I had to do was to purge myself of the memory of my homeland, to lobotomise the memory of Moscow, to ensure cockroaches no longer played with my hair. I had arrived and yet I felt I was departing.

I walked towards the bus; the driver was in the driver's seat, half asleep. I knocked on the door. The driver stirred slowly, he adjusted his glasses, his belly resting comfortably on the steering wheel. He had been eating what I later discovered to be KFC and he folded the brown bag and placed it in a bin bag on the side of his left knee. He sipped from a Diet Coke can and patted himself down. He then bent forward and fumbled with something and the door opened slowly.

'Are you travelling to Cardiff?' I asked.

He looked at me as if I had just asked a taboo question.

'Yes mate,' he said, repeating what the sign on the bus said, 'I am going to Swansea via Cardiff.'

Without noticing his sarcasm I continued, 'Can I have ticket to Cardiff?' I didn't know I was expected to say please or thank you.

'Would you like a one-way ticket or a return?' he asked.

What's with all the questions? I thought to myself, not knowing it was standard procedure.

'Can I have a single ticket to Cardiff?'

The driver then said, 'Please. That will be twenty-two pounds and I only accept cash.'

I counted out the money and handed it to the driver; he then issued me a ticket and said,

'Welcome aboard.'

There was nothing to be seen as we left London, except well-lit streets and darkness. I fell into a deep slumber.

*

I saw beautiful and ripe apple trees, I flew past the banana plantation of Molyko in Buea, I saw my sisters rejoicing, they were dancing the

Maboka dance, I saw the Small Soppo Development Association
Choir singing songs for my homecoming. I saw Fay, a poet, such
beauty she adorns, her thick African hair, I saw her smile, the
memory of her that 'suffices me less and less daily.' And in my flight,
I saw my mother. She was doing the zromelelele incantations,
thanking our ancestors.

*

We arrived in Cardiff at around seven-thirty in the morning and I
saw morning revellers making their way home, and bin men with
their machines ensuring the streets were clean. The devils had
roamed at night and now it was dawn, humans were coming out.

We stopped inside stand D2 in Cardiff Central Bus Station; I
knew we were in Cardiff as there was an announcement.

'We will soon be arriving in Cardiff, please make sure you have
all your belongings with you, and please put all your rubbish in
the bin bag at the front of the bus.'

'How lovely,' I thought. I was in a place with order and decorum,
with a way of doing things. Maybe Mola Francis was right about
the picture he had painted in our youthful minds.

I was hungry and wanted to eat the same KFC I saw the driver
disposing of in his bin bag, but I could not bring myself to ask him
about it. I don't think he liked me very much, as he thought I lacked
the etiquette and mannerism necessary for the environment in
which I now found myself. I looked around and I could see a small
kiosk at the other side of the bus station. When I got there, I bought
a packet of crisps, some Twix chocolate and a bottle of Fanta. I ate
and waited, still not knowing what to do or where to go.

Around nine o'clock, I noticed the buses started coming
frequently into the station; that was when I saw my first black
man—one of my people. I approached him and with my thick
Cameroonian accent, I said, 'Excuse me, do you know a
Cameroonian here called Francis?'

This guy looked at me like I had been smoking some sort of class-A drug. He spoke so fast the only thing I heard was the word Bristol. The guy then walked away and looked back at me shaking his head. I stood in front of the bus station munching on my crisps and sipping my Fanta. I saw another bus that had the word Barry Island written on it. Again I spotted a clean-shaven black guy and again I thought, *My people*.

'Do you know a Cameroonian called Francis?' I said.

This guy paced himself and looked at me before he started speaking in French. He said he was from Rwanda and that during the genocide between the Hutus and the Tutsis, in 1994, the Cameroonian Government had an open border policy to Rwandan refugees. He said although his mother was a casualty of the genocide, half of his family had settled in the southern part of Cameroon.

His name was Emmanuel Habimana and he took me to his house in Hunters Street in Barry Island. Three days later he took me to the immigration offices in Llanishen where I handed my passport to the officials telling them that I was a Cameroonian and not a Zimbabwean. The immigration officer was shocked when he looked at the passport and then looked back at me before saying, 'So tell me, Mr Eric Ngalle Charles, how the heck did you get past Heathrow airport?'

I arrived in Cardiff five months shy of my twenty-first birthday.

If you got this far reading this book, you have been reading of very dark times in my life, two years and two months spent in Russia, something that has been a burden for most of the time that I have been living in Wales and the UK. It has taken me the best part of nineteen years to be able to write down this very dark memory. I am still purging myself of it. I have had to organise myself in such a way that I know what can trigger what. I avoid these triggers. This story had to be told, especially with the situation in Cameroon right now, people are still falling victim of human trafficking on a grand scale. This book is a warning, many Cameroonians died in Russia, who knows how many are dying in Libya chasing that dream of going to the 'white man's land, the land of milk and honey'.

Afterword

As I sit on the fifth floor of Cardiff Central Library writing these memoirs, it is now 2017, eighteen years since arriving here in Wales. I received an email notification from the Arts Council of Wales "Dear Mr Charles, you have been awarded a Creative Wales Award... for your research into migration, memory and trauma." I shouted so loud, the security guard thinking something bad was happening rushed towards me before reminding me that shouting was not allowed. I walked towards the desk at the back and told my friend David who was on duty on that day. As I walked home, crossing the bridge towards Riverside and Grangetown, I thought of that day when I walked into my mother's kitchen, how she had been crying just before she handed me that letter summoning me to attend the courts in Buea as my dead father's will was being challenged by his family.

As I sit back and write, I remember those whom I have hurt along the way and for that, I am truly sorry. Today, here in Wales, I am celebrated as a writer, poet, playwright and actor but never at any time did I think I would live here, in the UK. I had my own plans, and the Gods... they had their own plans too.

I have been back to Cameroon three times. In 2018 I went back with Ifor ap Glyn, the National Poet of Wales and Mr Mike Jenkins, the Merthyr based poet and writer, with the help of Wales Arts International and together we have built a bridge between Wales and Cameroon, two countries I have grown to love for different reasons, one the country where half of my umbilical cord is buried and the other a country that gave me back my name, my voice, my identity and more importantly a platform.

For my mother and my siblings, this is the truth as to what happened in Russia; for my father's family, I loved you, and always will.

With Thanks

For the men and women here in Wales and in the UK who have guided my path, and have moulded me into becoming a successful writer, into settling here and making Wales my home, thank you very much. A special thanks to Professor Tom Cheesman, who has been not only a friend but a father figure, Sally Baker, Peter Florence for giving me a platform at the Hay Festival to showcase my work.

I am forever grateful to my friends and extended family in Ely, Deborah Green and the Green family in Ely for welcoming me, Avenue Hotspurs football team in Ely for buying me my first pair of football boots.

For my daughter and her sisters, this is how I came to be here in Wales.

PARTHIAN *Essays*

Notes from a Swing State
Writing from Wales and America
Zoë Brigley Thompson
ISBN 978-1-912681-29-7
£8.99 ● Paperback

'... startlingly beautiful imagery ...'
– Planet Magazine

Between the Boundaries
Adam Somerset
ISBN 978-1-912681-36-5
£8.99 ● Paperback

**'... accomplished collection which
engages, inspires and entertains.'**
– Jon Gower

Driving Home Both Ways
Dylan Moore
ISBN 978-1-912109-99-9
£8.99 ● Paperback

**Travel writing from the Creative Wales
Hay Festival International Fellow**

Seven Days
Nathan Munday
ISBN 978-1-912109-00-5
£8.99 ● Paperback

'...a beautiful, wise, and moving book.'

– Niall Griffiths

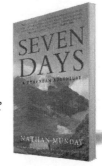

PARTHIAN

Parthian Books: New Fiction

The Blue Tent
Richard Gwyn
ISBN 978-1-912681-28-0
£9.99 ● Paperback

Author of Best-seller
The Colour of a Dog Running Away

Leading to Texas-2
Aled Smith
ISBN 978-1-912109-11-1
£8.99 ● Paperback

'Aled Smith has mixed a dark
and twisted filmic cocktail.'
– *Des Barry*

The Levels
Helen Pendry
ISBN 978-1-912109-40-1
£8.99 ● Paperback

A remarkable new vision set
in the hills of Wales...

Zero Hours
on the Boulevard
ed. Alexandra Büchler & Alison Evans
ISBN 978-1-912109-12-8
£8.99 ● Paperback

'A book about friendship,
community, identity and tribalism...'
– *New Welsh Review*

PARTHIAN